Cadbury's
CHOCOLATE
COOKBOOK

Cadbury's
CHOCOLATE
COOKBOOK

PATRICIA DUNBAR

CHANCELLOR
PRESS

CONTENTS

All photography by the photographic department
Cadbury Schweppes, Bournville, Birmingham

*The author and publisher would like to thank the following for kindly
supplying some of the accessories used in the colour photographs:*
Royal Doulton: page 15
A. Tullet & Sons, Northfield, Birmingham: pages 43 and 119
Dartington Glass: pages 83 and 111
P. Lyons & Co, Stirchley, Birmingham: page 63

Acknowledgement
I could not possibly have prepared this book without the help of my
team of home economists, past and present. I should particularly like to
thank Kate, Bridget, Frances and Jenny whose ideas have always been
appreciated, and Carole for typing it all.

First published in Great Britain in 1978 by Hamlyn

This edition published in 1993 by Chancellor Press
an imprint of Reed Consumer Books Limited
Michelin House, 81 Fulham Road, London SW3 6RB
and Auckland, Melbourne, Singapore and Toronto

Reprinted 1993

Copyright © Cadbury Typhoo Limited 1978

ISBN 1 85152 253 0

A CIP catalogue record for this book is available from the British Library

Printed in China

Line drawings by Susan Neale

USEFUL FACTS AND FIGURES

Oven temperatures

The table below gives recommended equivalents.

	°C	°F	Gas Mark
Very cool	110	225	$\frac{1}{4}$
	120	250	$\frac{1}{2}$
Cool or Slow	140	275	1
	150	300	2
Warm	160	325	3
Moderate	180	350	4
Moderately hot	190	375	5
Fairly hot	200	400	6
Hot	220	425	7
Very hot	230	450	8
	240	475	9

An Imperial/American guide to solid and liquid measures

Solid measures

IMPERIAL	AMERICAN
1 lb butter or margarine	2 cups
1 lb flour	4 cups
1 lb granulated or caster sugar	2 cups
1 lb icing sugar	3 cups
8 oz rice	1 cup

Liquid measures

IMPERIAL	AMERICAN
$\frac{1}{4}$ pint liquid	$\frac{2}{3}$ cup liquid
$\frac{1}{2}$ pint	$1\frac{1}{4}$ cups
$\frac{3}{4}$ pint	2 cups
1 pint	$2\frac{1}{2}$ cups
$1\frac{1}{2}$ pints	$3\frac{3}{4}$ cups
2 pints	5 cups ($2\frac{1}{2}$ pints)

Notes for American and Australian users

In America the 8-oz measuring cup is used. In Australia metric measures are now used in conjunction with the standard 250-ml measuring cup. The imperial pint, used in Britain and Australia, is 20 fl oz, while the American pint is 16 fl oz. It is important to remember that the Australian tablespoon differs from both the British and American tablespoons; the table below gives a comparison. The British standard tablespoon, which has been used throughout this book, holds 17.7 ml, the American 14.2 ml, and the Australian 20 ml. A teaspoon holds approximately 5 ml in all three countries.

NOTE: WHEN MAKING ANY OF THE RECIPES IN THIS BOOK, ONLY FOLLOW ONE SET OF MEASURES AS THEY ARE NOT INTERCHANGEABLE

Spoon measures All spoon measures given in this book are level unless otherwise stated.

Can sizes At present, cans are marked with the exact (usually to the nearest whole number) metric equivalent of the imperial weight of the contents, so we have followed this practice when giving can sizes.

Gelatine One envelope of powdered gelatine equals 14 g/$\frac{1}{2}$ oz.

British	American	Australian
1 teaspoon	1 teaspoon	1 teaspoon
1 tablespoon	1 tablespoon	1 tablespoon
2 tablespoons	3 tablespoons	2 tablespoons
$3\frac{1}{2}$ tablespoons	4 tablespoons	3 tablespoons
4 tablespoons	5 tablespoons	$3\frac{1}{2}$ tablespoons

 Denotes freezing instructions.
 Denotes Cook's Tip.

THE STORY OF CHOCOLATE

How it all started

In 1824 a young Quaker, John Cadbury, opened a shop in Birmingham mainly to sell tea and coffee. But he sold certain other things too, as he pointed out in his first advertisement in the Birmingham Gazette on March 1, 1824. 'J.C. is desirous of introducing to particular notice "Cocoa Nibs", prepared by himself, an article affording a most nutritious beverage for breakfast.'

His venture into cocoa was to have far-reaching effects. From a one-man business, the firm of Cadbury Schweppes has become one of the leading food, confectionery and beverage manufacturers in the UK.

Cadbury has revolutionised the eating habits of millions of people. And it all started in the cellar of that small Birmingham shop. Here John Cadbury experimented in the grinding of cocoa beans with a pestle and mortar and found that he could sell more cocoa and drinking chocolate made to his own Cadbury recipe than the unground 'nibs' mentioned in that original advertisement. He mastered the essentials of cocoa and chocolate making which he and his successors were to develop and perfect.

In 1822 only a total of 126 tons of cocoa beans were imported into Britain. Nowadays Cadbury is one of the world's major buyers of cocoa, purchasing over 60,000 tons a year.

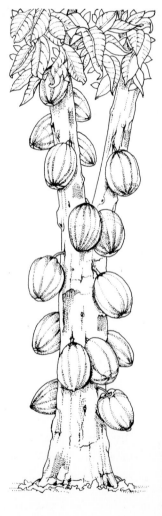

The cultivation of cocoa

Cocoa and chocolate are both derived from the cocoa bean, which grows in pods on the cocoa tree, or *Theobroma cacao*.

The cocoa tree originated in the Amazon forests and now grows as far apart as West Africa and Malaya. The trees can only be cultivated in conditions similar to those of its natural habitat. The climate must be neither too dry nor too cold and there must be shelter from the winds.

In 1879, the first cocoa beans were planted in the Gold Coast, now known as Ghana. Today, West Africa produces about 60% of the world's supply of cocoa, with 30% from South America. The remainder comes from several other countries.

Sometimes the young trees are grown from seeds planted by the cocoa farmer. More usually the seeds are grown in special nurseries and then transplanted in the cocoa farm. The

Cocoa pods, showing beans inside

trees start bearing fruit when they are four or five years old. In shape and size, they resemble an English apple tree but have broad, luxuriant leaves, and the fruit or pods grow from both the trunk and branches. Inside each pod are 20 to 40 seeds like plump almonds and covered by a sweet, white pulp. These seeds are the cocoa beans.

In West Africa, the pods are harvested during the last three months of the year. The pulp and seeds are scooped out and formed into a heap on a layer of large leaves. More leaves are used to cover the heap to keep off the rain and keep in the warmth. The fermentation which now takes place is a vital stage in the cocoa and chocolate making process, developing chocolate flavour as we know it and removing the astringency of the unfermented bean. The fermentation process takes five or six days and the contents of the heap must be turned from time to time as it proceeds. (Sometimes fermentation is carried out in a cascade of boxes and the beans are dropped from one box to another to attain this mixing.) During fermentation, alcohol and acidic, vinegar-like liquids are produced and drain away and the temperature rises to about 50°C/122°F. When fermentation is complete, the wet mass of beans is dried, usually by being spread out in the sun.

The dried and fermented beans are packed into bags containing about 63 kg. Samples are drawn for inspection and grading. Some beans are cut open and the colour determines whether fermentation has been carried out correctly—a well-fermented bean has a characteristic chocolate brown colour. Checks are also made for defects such as mould or damage by insects.

Gathering the pods

Sacks of beans are stored in dockside warehouses until required for shipment. All beans used by Cadbury in the United Kingdom are processed in one of the world's most modern cocoa processing plants situated at Chirk in North Wales.

Historical background

Cocoa was first introduced into England during the seventeenth century. But the Aztecs in Central America had been drinking chocolate hundreds of years before the Spanish explorer Cortez conquered Mexico in 1519. They called it 'chocolatl'. Cortez is said to have tasted his first drinking chocolate in a golden goblet in the palace of the Aztec Emperor, Montezuma. It must have been a rather bitter, pungent drink for the Spaniards improved the flavour by adding sugar and guarded the secret of its preparation for almost a century.

When it was finally introduced into the courts of Spain, Italy, Germany, France and England, chocolate remained an expensive luxury. When the first chocolate house opened in London in 1657, chocolate cost from 50 pence to 75 pence a pound in weight (when the pound sterling was worth far more than in the 1970s) and the high price was sustained for many years by heavy import duties.

It remained a luxury product until Gladstone's time when, in 1853, he lowered the duty to a uniform rate of one old penny per pound. In the early days, it was sold by auction in London. Producers sent samples to manufacturers who roasted and tested the beans and then bid for the variety they preferred. Auctions were known as 'sales by candle'. This was derived from the practice of having a lighted candle with pins stuck at intervals down its side on the auctioneer's desk. The last bid before the pin fell out secured the cocoa beans.

The manufacture of cocoa and chocolate

The cocoa we buy from the local shop is made from cocoa nibs roasted and ground, from which a portion of the cocoa butter has been removed. It takes a whole year's crop from one tree on a cocoa farm to make 454 grams/1 lb of cocoa. Chocolate is made by adding extra cocoa butter and sugar to ground cocoa nibs. In the manufacture of milk chocolate, milk is also added.

In at least two essentials, roasting and winnowing, modern methods of making cocoa and chocolate are similar to those followed by the Mexicans and Peruvians centuries ago.

Chocolate for eating was unknown until early Victorian times and the primitive recipes were only concerned with making a drink from cocoa beans. These were first roasted, generally in earthen pots, then winnowed in the wind to remove the shells. Afterwards they were ground either between two stones or with a stone rolling pin on a stone slab.

These homely methods have become far more sophisticated in the transition to large-scale production and there is no doubt that the finest drinking and eating chocolates of today are vastly superior to anything tasted either by the Victorians or the ancient Peruvians.

Cleaning and Roasting: When the cocoa beans arrive at the factory they are sorted and cleaned. The beans are then roasted in revolving drums. It is through this roasting that the bean takes on its characteristic flavour and aroma, and the shell becomes brittle. Roasting time is about an hour at an effective temperature of 135°C/275°F.

8

Kibbling and Winnowing: The roasted beans are then broken down into small fragments (kibbled) in preparation for winnowing. In the winnower, the brittle shell is blown away by an 'artificial wind', leaving behind the broken cotyledon of the beans, known in the industry as 'nibs'.

Extraction of cocoa butter: The nibs are ground between steel rollers until the friction and heat of milling gradually reduces it to a thick, chocolate-coloured liquid with the consistency of thick cream. The cocoa nib emerges as liquid, not powder, because it contains about 55% cocoa butter. The mixture is now called 'mass' and solidifies on cooling. This 'mass' is the basis of all chocolate and cocoa products, i.e. Bournville Cocoa, Drinking Chocolate and chocolate confectionery.

Cocoa is made by extracting some of the cocoa butter from it, otherwise it would be too rich to make a palatable drink. About half of the cocoa butter is pressed out leaving a solid block of cocoa. To produce fine high grade cocoa, this is ground and reground until it can be sieved through a fine gauze. Samples are tested in the quality control laboratory.

How chocolate is made

The 'mass' goes straight to the Bournville chocolate factory for the production of plain chocolate. It is different for Dairy Milk Chocolate. Here the 'mass' is sent to 'milk factories' at Marlbrook in the county of Hereford and Worcester and Frampton in Gloucestershire, where it is mixed with fresh full cream milk and sugar which has been condensed into a rich creamy liquid.

This chocolate flavoured condensed milk is then dried in vacuum ovens to give milk chocolate 'crumb' which is taken to the chocolate factories at Bournville and Somerdale.

The Chocolate Factory is the final stage where extra cocoa butter is added to help the processing for the moulding into the familiar bars. After being ground and mixed, both plain and milk chocolate undergo a final pummelling treatment known as 'conching' which gives Cadbury's chocolate its famous smoothness.

After 'conching', chocolate can either be moulded into blocks of, for example, Cadbury's Dairy Milk Chocolate or extra cocoa butter can be added to make it more fluid for use in covering chocolate biscuits or in confectionery.

Melting chocolate: Place the bar of Bournville plain chocolate whole, or broken into squares, in a bowl suspended over a pan of hot, not boiling, water. Leave to melt.

Making chocolate leaves: Choose unblemished rose leaves. Dip leaves into melted Bournville plain chocolate, coating the veined side. Place on waxed paper. When dry, carefully peel away the leaf.

Making chocolate shapes: Trace outlines on plain paper. Cover with waxed paper. Fill a greaseproof paper piping bag with melted chocolate and follow the shape. Fill in centres as necessary.

Peel off the waxed paper carefully. If the chocolate hardens in the bag, heat in the oven or over hot water until softened. Store shapes in an airtight container.

Making chocolate curls: Scrape a vegetable peeler along the flat side of a bar of Bournville plain chocolate, shaving it off into curls. Handle carefully. Alternatively, grate coarsely.

Making chocolate caraque: Spread melted Bournville plain chocolate on to Formica or marble. Leave to set. Using a sharp knife, scrape the chocolate, allowing it to peel off into long curls.

Making chocolate cut-outs: Spread melted Bournville plain chocolate thickly on waxed paper. Leave to set. Cut out shapes with cocktail cutters. Any chocolate remaining may be melted for use again.

Making chocolate squares or triangles: Spread melted Bournville plain chocolate into a rectangle and set. Use a ruler to mark into even-sized squares. Cut squares diagonally for triangles. Cut with a sharp knife.

CHOCOLATE COOKERY

Both Bournville Plain and Dairy Milk Chocolate depend to a large extent on cocoa butter for their flavour and characteristic eating qualities. The so-called 'cooking chocolates' usually do not meet the United Kingdom legal definition for cocoa and chocolate products, and therefore have to be suitably labelled. The cocoa butter has been replaced with other fats such as coconut and palm kernel oils, which alters the melting properties to the detriment of the flavour. Some cocoa powder is usually included in these 'cooking chocolates'. Other essences and edible fillers are often added as they are cheaper than the product of the natural cocoa bean.

Cocoa is the most economical chocolate flavour for use in cookery. When a high proportion of starch ingredients are used, such as flour and cornflour, it is generally better to sieve the cocoa in with the dry ingredients. Cocoa is also better when the mixture is to be thoroughly cooked, such as in cakes, biscuits, puddings and sauces. In other recipes, the starch cells should preferably be broken down before cooking. A practical way to do this is by the addition of enough boiling water to the cocoa to make a thick paste. This also enables the cocoa to be easily blended into a recipe.

Drinking Chocolate produces a milder flavour and is sweeter, containing a high proportion of sugar with the cocoa. When used in a recipe, the sugar quantities have to be adapted and generally lowered to counteract the extra sweetness. As the name implies, Drinking Chocolate is particularly suitable for milk drinks.

Cadbury's Flake is made from milk chocolate which is compressed so that thin layers roll against each other, forming flakes. These are then cut into lengths. Flakes are often served with ice cream but can be most useful for cake decorating and in other recipes. Buttons are made from milk chocolate.

Nutrition Chocolate confectionery is classed amongst the most valuable of foods. The high concentration of nutrients can easily be assimilated by the body and are consequently a most suitable food for those taking a great deal of exercise. 28 g/1 oz of plain chocolate provides about one-twelfth the daily requirement of iron in the diet.

Multiply the amount of Calories by 4.2 to obtain the approximate conversion to kilojoules.

Composition of Bournville Cocoa per 28 g/1 oz

Calories	130
Protein	6.5 g
Fats	6.0 g
Carbohydrates	13.0 g
Calcium	40.0 mg
Iron	3.0 mg
Sodium	412.0 mg

Composition of Bournville Plain Chocolate per 28 g/1 oz

Calories	144
Protein	1.1 g
Fats	8.3 g
Carbohydrates	17.3 g
Calcium	8.4 mg
Iron	0.7 mg
Sodium	6.2 mg

Cocoa and chocolate also contain other mineral salts, e.g. phosphorus and potassium, in amounts comparable with many other foods. The milk in milk chocolate adds valuable calcium.

CAKES FOR ALL OCCASIONS

Think of a chocolate recipe, think of a cake. There are endless variations and most cooks have their own favourite recipe. We have included a selection which range from the plain and simple to the luscious iced layer cakes. Careful preparation and cooking is important; weigh and measure ingredients accurately for perfect results every time.

Novelty cakes, which make the centre-piece for a child's birthday party or similar occasion, feature in this chapter. Children look forward to their own special cake on the great day, and their pleasure is worth the extra time and effort. Birthday cakes are expensive to buy and home-made ones certainly work out cheaper, as well as being more rewarding.

Victoria Sandwich Cake

※

The cakes should be packed with a piece of greaseproof paper between the layers, then wrapped, sealed and labelled.

A 2-egg quantity of the cake mixture can be made in two sandwich tins measuring 15–18 cm/6–7 inches. If preferred, plain flour can be used, allowing 5 ml/1 teaspoon of baking powder to every 50 g/2 oz of the flour and cocoa weighed together.

Metric		Imperial
175 g	margarine	6 oz
175 g	caster sugar	6 oz
3	eggs	3
150 g	self-raising flour	6 oz
25 g	Bournville cocoa	1 oz
	greaseproof paper	
2 19-cm	shallow cake tins	2 7½-inch

Prepare the cake tins first. Cut two circles of greaseproof paper the same size as the tins. Grease the tins, put in the paper circles and grease these also.

Cream the margarine with the sugar really well. This can easily be done with an electric mixer. Add the eggs one at a time with 5 ml/1 teaspoon of the flour. Sieve the flour and cocoa together and fold into the mixture. Add a little milk if the mixture is too dry, which will depend on the size of the eggs. Divide the mixture between the tins. Smooth over the surface with a palette knife, hollowing out the centre slightly so that the cakes will rise evenly. Bake in the centre of a moderately hot oven (190°C, 375°F, Gas Mark 5) for 25–30 minutes until the cakes spring back when touched. Turn the cakes out on to a wire rack and remove the paper circles. Immediately turn the cakes over again so that there will not be marks from the wire on top. Leave to cool. Later, sandwich with butter icing and decorate.

13

One-Stage Cake

Use soft margarine and add 5 ml/1 teaspoon baking powder to the ingredients for the Victoria sandwich cake. Beat all the ingredients together for at least 2 minutes until they are thoroughly mixed. Bake as usual.

Chocolate Butter Icing

Metric		Imperial
100 g	**butter**	4 oz
150–225 g	**icing sugar, sieved**	6–8 oz
60 ml	**Bournville cocoa**	2 tablespoons
80 ml	**boiling water**	4 tablespoons
	flavouring essence (optional)	

Warm the butter in a bowl if it is really hard. Beat until softened then cream with the sieved icing sugar until the mixture is a nice light colour and texture. Dissolve the cocoa in the boiling water then beat it into the butter.

A few drops of a flavouring essence such as peppermint, orange, coffee or vanilla may be added for variety.

Store the butter icing in a covered container in the refrigerator or freezer.

Plain Butter Icing

Make as for Chocolate Butter Icing but omit the cocoa. Add a few drops of vanilla essence for a vanilla flavoured butter icing.

Glacé Icing

Metric		Imperial
225 g	**icing sugar, sieved**	8 oz
about 40 ml	**warm water**	about 2 tablespoons
	or fruit juice	

Combine icing sugar and water in a bowl and beat with a wooden spoon until smooth. Use immediately.

To make a greaseproof paper piping bag

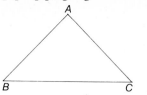

1 Cut a square of greaseproof paper at least 25 cm/10 inches in diameter, fold in half diagonally, forming a triangle. Make a small slit in the centre of the folded line to help give a sharper point.

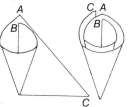

2 Take corner (B) and roll it so that it lies inside the corner (A).

3 Bring corner (C) round the outside of the bag so that it lies exactly behind (A).

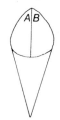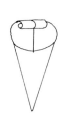

4 Adjust paper so that all corners are together and there is a sharp tip to the bag.
5 Fold over point (A) two or three times to keep bag together.
6 If an icing pipe is used, snip a small piece off the point and drop in selected pipe. To use the bag on its own, fill with icing then cut off tip.

Victoria Sandwich Variations:
Chocolate Cake (see page 16);
Mocha Cake (see page 16);
Sunshine Fruit Ring (see page 18); Christmas Tree Sparkle (see page 18); Button Cake (see page 17); Feather Iced Cake (see page 17)

Victoria Sandwich Variations

Illustrated on page 15

Chocolate Cake

Metric		Imperial
1	**chocolate Victoria sandwich cake**	1
	double quantity chocolate butter icing	
	(see page 14)	
7	**Bournville plain chocolate**	7
	triangles (see page 11)	
	piping bag and star pipe	

Sandwich the cakes together with the butter icing and spread it over the top and sides of the cake. Put the remainder into the piping bag. Mark a semi-circle on top of the cake and fill this in with stars of icing. Pipe stars round the top and bottom edges too, or a rope pattern. Stick the chocolate triangles into half the cake (as illustrated) and dust with icing sugar.

Mocha Cake

Metric		Imperial
1	**chocolate Victoria sandwich cake**	1
about 10 ml	**instant coffee powder**	about 2 teaspoons
550 g	**vanilla butter icing**	1 lb 4 oz
	(see page 14)	
3 squares	**Bournville plain chocolate**	3 squares
15 ml	**coffee beans**	1 tablespoon

greaseproof paper piping bag

Alternatively, the cake filling can be chocolate flavoured, leaving the remainder of the icing coffee flavoured.

Dissolve the coffee in a little boiling water and mix it into the butter icing. Sandwich the cakes together with some of the coffee butter icing.

Cover the top and sides with a thick layer of icing. Make a ribbed pattern round the side by drawing a scraper with a serrated edge along the butter icing, or use a fork for a similar effect. Put the cake on to a plate. Mark into eight sections. Decorate with stars round the top and bottom and one in the centre. Melt the chocolate in a small bowl over hot water, put in a paper piping bag and cut off the tip. Make an 'S' shape pattern on each of the sections. Complete the cake by putting a roasted coffee bean on to each star; these can be eaten.

Feather Iced Cake

Metric		Imperial
I	**chocolate Victoria sandwich cake**	I
	vanilla or chocolate flavoured	
	butter icing (see page 14)	
about 40 ml	**warm water**	about 2 tablespoons
225 g	**icing sugar, sieved**	8 oz
60 ml	**Cadbury's chocolate spread**	4 tablespoons
I	**glacé cherry**	I
50 g	**chopped nuts**	2 oz

greaseproof paper piping bag

Sandwich the cake layers together with butter icing and spread some round the edge. Beat sufficient warm water into the sieved icing sugar to make a fairly thick spreading consistency. Spread this over the top of the cake with a palette knife. Do not lift the knife or cake crumbs will be mixed into the icing. The icing can drip down the sides. Quickly mix a little hot water into the chocolate spread to make it pliable. Fill the piping bag, snip off the end and pipe evenly spaced lines across the top of the cake, in the wet glacé icing. Draw a skewer backwards and forwards, across the chocolate lines, making the feathering effect. This can be done in a fan shape, with the cherry at the base. Press the chopped nuts in to the sides of the cake and leave the icing to set.

To get a good finish with feather icing, work quickly so that the glacé icing does not form a skin before the lines are piped. Thin chocolate glacé icing may be used for the lines, which should be spaced evenly apart for a neat appearance.

Button Cake

Metric		Imperial
I	**chocolate Victoria sandwich cake**	I
	vanilla butter icing (see page 14)	
I	**packet Cadbury's Buttons**	I

Sandwich the cakes with butter icing and spread it over the top. Mark lines with a fork in both directions so that there is a trellis effect. Stick the Buttons in at an angle round the edge.

Sunshine Fruit Ring

Metric		Imperial
I	chocolate Victoria sandwich cake	I
175 g	pineapple jam	6 oz
50 g	flaked almonds, browned	2 oz
227-g	can pineapple rings	8-oz
298-g	mandarin oranges	10½-oz
15 ml	arrowroot	3 teaspoons

Sandwich the cakes together with jam and also spread it over the sides. Roll the cake in the almonds to coat the sides. Lift on to a plate. Drain the juice from the fruit and reserve. Arrange the pineapple rings, cut into pieces, with the mandarin oranges to make an attractive pattern on the top. Blend the arrowroot with a little of the fruit juice then bring it to the boil with about 250 ml/¼ pint of juice, stirring continuously. Cover the fruit with the cold glaze.

Christmas Tree Sparkle

Metric		Imperial
I	chocolate Victoria sandwich cake	I
175 g	butter	6 oz
375 g	icing sugar, sieved	12 oz
5 ml	vanilla essence	I teaspoon
40 ml	Bournville cocoa	2 tablespoons
2	Cadbury's Flakes	2
I	packet Cadbury's Buttons	I
	silver or coloured sugar balls	

piping bag and star pipe

To make the icing, cream the butter with the sieved icing sugar and vanilla essence. Using half the amount, sandwich the cakes together and spread a smooth layer on top. Mix the cocoa with a little boiling water and beat this paste into the remaining butter icing. Coat the sides of the cake, reserving some icing for a decorative edging. Crush the Flakes in the wrapping and press the pieces into the butter icing round the sides. Using a piping bag with a star pipe attached, pipe an edge of chocolate butter icing round the top. Practice making a Christmas tree shape with the Buttons and silver balls on the table before transferring it to the centre of the cake. Lift on to a plate or cake board.

Desert Fort Cake (see page 20)

Desert Fort Cake

Illustrated on page 19

Metric		Imperial
325 g	**margarine**	12 oz
325 g	**caster sugar**	12 oz
6	**eggs**	6
325 g	**self-raising flour, sieved**	12 oz
25 g	**Bournville cocoa, sieved**	1 oz
50 g	**ground almonds**	2 oz
	Icing	
450 g	**chocolate butter icing**	1 lb
	(double quantity recipe, see page 14)	
	Decoration	
150 g	**chocolate finger biscuits**	$5\frac{1}{4}$ oz
	soft brown sugar	
	toy soldiers and flags	
25-cm	**square cake tin, greased and lined**	10-inch
30-cm	**square cake board**	12-inch

Use an electric mixer for making this large amount of mixture, if available. Beat the margarine and sugar together until they are thoroughly mixed and smooth. Add the eggs one at a time by hand, with a little of the sieved flour and cocoa. Fold in the remaining dry ingredients, including the ground almonds. Add a little milk if necessary to make a dropping consistency. Turn the mixture into the prepared tin, hollow out the centre so that when the cake rises, it will be flat. Bake in a moderately hot oven (190°C, 375°F, Gas Mark 5) for about 45 minutes. Test with a warm skewer to see if it is cooked through. Cover with a piece of paper if the cake seems to be getting too brown. Cool in the tin slightly before turning out on to a wire tray.

Prepare the chocolate butter icing. Carefully measure a 13-cm/5-inch square in the centre of the cake and cut it out. Cut the centre square into four, making smaller squares. Lift the larger square carefully on to the centre of the cake board. Stick the smaller squares on to each of the corners, with butter icing, to make the 'turrets'. Very carefully, spread the whole cake, inside and out, with the butter icing, making it as smooth as possible.

Divide the finger biscuits into four. Stand them up between the 'turrets', pressing them into the icing. Sprinkle soft brown sugar in the centre and round the edge to represent the 'sand'. Arrange the soldiers and flags on the 'fort'. Birthday candles may be stuck into the 'turrets'.

The cake may be frozen undecorated, or when covered with the butter icing, without the finger biscuits or decorations. Pack carefully, seal and label. Open freeze first if decorated.

If you have an oven that bakes very evenly, it is probably unnecessary to line the cake tin completely. With a cake this size, a paper lining helps to prevent the edges from burning. Warm the mixer bowl and beater before beginning.

Butterscotch Cake

Freeze the complete cake. Pack carefully, seal and label.

Substitute the milk in the frosting for some of the evaporated milk in the cake recipe, which makes an even creamier frosting. Make up the difference with water in the cake.

Metric		Imperial
200 g	**self-raising flour**	7 oz
2.5 ml	**salt**	$\frac{1}{2}$ teaspoon
40 ml	**Bournville cocoa**	2 tablespoons
225 g	**caster sugar**	8 oz
100 g	**soft margarine**	4 oz
2	**eggs**	2
1	**small can evaporated milk**	1
5 ml	**vanilla essence**	1 teaspoon
	Frosting	
100 g	**butter**	4 oz
100 g	**soft brown sugar**	4 oz
60 ml	**milk**	3 tablespoons
5 ml	**vanilla essence**	1 teaspoon
300 g	**icing sugar**	12 oz
2 18-cm	**round shallow cake tins, greased and base lined**	2 7-inch

Sieve the flour, salt and cocoa together. Add the sugar. Rub in the margarine. Beat the eggs with the evaporated milk and vanilla essence then beat the liquid into the dry ingredients, rather like making a batter. When it is thoroughly mixed, divide the soft cake mixture evenly between the tins and smooth over the surfaces. Bake in a moderate oven (180°C, 350°F, Gas Mark 4) for 35–40 minutes. Turn out to cool on a wire tray.

To make the frosting, place the butter and sugar in a pan. Stir gently and cook over a low heat until it comes to the boil. Take the pan off the heat, add the milk and the vanilla essence. Sieve the icing sugar into a bowl. Beat in the melted ingredients and continue beating until the frosting is really smooth and quite thick. Sandwich the cakes together with about one-third of the amount and cover the cake with the remainder. Make swirls in the frosting with a knife or teaspoon. Lift on to a plate.

Flake Slice

Illustrated opposite

Metric		Imperial
3 size 2	**eggs**	3 large
75 g	**caster sugar**	3 oz
50 g	**butter**	2 oz
75 g	**plain flour, sieved**	3 oz
	sherry or fruit juice	
	Icing	
125 g	**butter**	4 oz
25 g	**Bournville cocoa**	1 oz
200 g	**icing sugar, sieved**	7 oz
	Decoration	
50 g	**Bournville plain chocolate**	2 oz
4	**large Cadbury's Flakes**	4
4	**glacé cherries, halved**	4
28-cm × 18-cm	**cake tin,**	11-inch × 7-inch
	greased and base lined	
	greaseproof paper piping bag	

Whisk the eggs and sugar together in a fairly large bowl, over a pan of hot water. An electric mixer may be used instead. Whisk until the mixture is stiff enough to leave a good trail. Gently melt the butter. Fold in the sieved flour with the butter, making sure that no pockets of flour remain. Pour into the prepared tin. Bake in a fairly hot oven (200°C, 400°F, Gas Mark 6) for about 20 minutes until the cake is cooked and springy when touched. Turn out and cool on a wire tray.

Slice the cake lengthways through the middle then again lengthways, making four long strips of cake. Moisten these with a little sherry or fruit juice.

To make the icing, cream the butter well. Blend the cocoa with enough boiling water to make a stiff paste then add to the butter. Beat in the sieved icing sugar. Pile the cake layers on top of each other with a layer of butter icing in between each. Spread it over the top and on the sides too.

Grate the chocolate and cover the sides and the ends of the cake with it. Melt the remaining grated chocolate in a small bowl over hot water. Put the chocolate into a small paper piping bag. Cut each of the Flakes in half with a sharp knife. Arrange the halved Flakes evenly down the centre of the cake, with half a glacé cherry in between. Zigzag lines of chocolate over the top. Lift the cake on to a plate or board.

Freeze the cake and butter icing but omit the Flake and chocolate decoration. Pack, seal and label.

Crumbled Flake can be used to coat the sides of the cake, instead of the grated chocolate. This will give a rougher texture.

Cherry Sparkle (see page 25);
Bournvita Loaf (see page 24);
Flake Slice (see above)

Bournvita Loaf

Illustrated on page 23

Metric		Imperial
200 g	self-raising flour	8 oz
	pinch of salt	
50 g	Bournvita	2 oz
50 g	soft brown sugar	2 oz
50 g	mixed dried fruit	2 oz
50 g	stoned dates	2 oz
40 ml	golden syrup	2 tablespoons
125 ml	milk	¼ pint
0.5-kg	loaf tin,	1-lb
	greased and base lined	

Sieve the flour with the salt. Mix in the Bournvita, sugar and dried fruit. Chop the dates then add them too. Using a hot spoon, measure the syrup into the mixture and add enough milk to make a soft dropping consistency. Turn into the prepared tin, level the surface and bake in a moderate oven (180°C, 350°F, Gas Mark 4) for 50–60 minutes. Test with a warm skewer to see that the loaf is cooked. Cool in the tin and turn out later. Peel off the greaseproof paper.

Serve in slices with butter.

Wrap the loaf in foil or a polythene bag, seal and label. Freeze for up to 3 months. Defrost at room temperature, for about 4 hours.

Do not open the oven door until the minimum cooking time is completed. A draught can cause the loaf to sink in the middle. This loaf keeps well in an airtight tin.

Crusted Marble Cake

Illustrated on page 31

Metric		Imperial
175 g	margarine	6 oz
175 g	caster sugar	6 oz
3	eggs	3
125 g	plain flour	5 oz
15 ml	baking powder	3 teaspoons
2.5 ml	vanilla essence	½ teaspoon
25 g	Bournville cocoa, sieved	1 oz
20 ml	milk	1 tablespoon
75 g	Bournville plain chocolate	3 oz
18-cm	square deep cake tin,	7-inch
	greased and base lined	

Beat the margarine and sugar well together, and add the eggs one at a time. Sieve the flour and baking powder together

Wrap, seal, label then freeze the cake complete.

Self-raising flour can be used instead of the flour and baking powder. If a square cake tin is not available, use a 19-cm/7½-inch round deep tin. The cake can be left whole or cut into pieces when cool.

and fold into the mixture. Put half the mixture into another bowl. Mix the vanilla essence into one amount and the sieved cocoa and the milk into the other, making sure they are thoroughly mixed. Place alternate spoonsful of the different coloured cake mixture in the prepared tin. Carefully smooth over the top and hollow out the centre.

Melt the chocolate in a bowl over hot water. Spread the chocolate over the chocolate cake mixture in the tin but do not worry if it spreads a little. Bake in a moderately hot oven (190°C, 375°F, Gas Mark 5) for about 40 minutes. Leave the cake in the tin just long enough for the chocolate to harden enough to handle then turn out on to a wire tray to cool.

Cherry Sparkle

Illustrated on page 23

The cake would be better frozen without the topping. Wrap, seal and label. Prepare the topping while the cake is defrosting and if it is really hot, it will stick satisfactorily.

This one-stage method is excellent but a good result depends on beating the ingredients really well together.

Metric		Imperial
175 g	**self-raising flour**	6 oz
25 g	**Bournville cocoa**	1 oz
5 ml	**baking powder**	1 teaspoon
175 g	**soft margarine**	6 oz
175 g	**caster sugar**	6 oz
3	**eggs**	3
	Topping	
100 g	**glacé cherries**	4 oz
50 g	**walnut halves**	2 oz
100 g	**pineapple or apricot jam**	4 oz
	greaseproof paper	
1-kg	**loaf tin, greased**	2-lb

Cut a double piece of greaseproof paper to fit the width of the tin, allowing a bit extra at either end. Lay this in the tin and grease the paper.

Sieve the flour with the cocoa and baking powder into a bowl. Add the margarine, sugar and eggs, and cream thoroughly until well blended. Spoon the mixture into the prepared tin, hollow out the centre slightly and level off the surface. Bake in a moderate oven (180°C, 350°F, Gas Mark 4) for 50–60 minutes. Poke a skewer into the centre and if it comes out clean, the cake is ready.

While the cake is cooking, prepare the topping. Halve the cherries and put them into a pan with the walnuts and jam. Stir continuously and bring to the boil. Spread this mixture on top of the cake immediately it comes out of the oven. Leave in the tin to cool then carefully lift the cake out.

Tipsy Cake

Metric		Imperial
100 g	**Bournville plain chocolate**	4 oz
175 g	*margarine*	6 oz
175 g	caster sugar	6 oz
3	eggs	3
175 g	**self-raising flour, sieved**	6 oz
	pinch of salt	
	vanilla essence	
100 g	**granulated sugar**	4 oz
120 ml	**water**	6 tablespoons
40–60 ml	**brandy, rum or sherry**	2–3 tablespoons
275 ml	· **whipping cream**	$\frac{1}{2}$ pint
1 tablespoon	caster sugar	1 tablespoon
2 20-cm	**round shallow cake tins,**	2 8-inch
	greased and base lined	
	piping bag and star pipe	

Melt the chocolate in a bowl over a pan of hot water. When melted, spread half quite thickly on to waxed paper and leave to set again. Keep the remaining chocolate melted.

Cream the margarine and sugar together. Gradually beat in the eggs one at a time and fold in the sieved flour with a pinch of salt. Halve the mixture between two bowls and add a few drops of vanilla essence to one amount. Mix the melted chocolate into the other. Place alternate spoonsful of the vanilla and chocolate cake mixture in the prepared tins, dividing it between both tins. Swirl the colours together slightly and smooth over the top, hollowing out the centre slightly. Bake the cakes in a moderately hot oven (190°C, 375°F, Gas Mark 5) for about 25 minutes. Turn the cakes out on to a wire tray to cool.

Dissolve the granulated sugar in the water over gentle heat. When the sugar crystals have disappeared, increase the heat and boil rapidly for about 3 minutes. Take the syrup off the heat and cool slightly before adding the brandy. Pour over the cakes just before they are to be assembled.

With a sharp knife, cut the set chocolate into 3.5-cm/ 1$\frac{1}{2}$-inch squares; you will need at least 4 good ones but any extra will keep in a screwtop jar. Cut the squares across into 2 triangles. Whip the cream until it will hold its shape then fold in the tablespoon of caster sugar. Pipe a circle of rosettes round the edge of one cake, upside-down so that the marbled pattern shows. Sandwich the cakes together with the remaining cream. Place the chocolate triangles in position.

It may be easier to freeze the cake layers without the cream. Place a sheet of greaseproof or waxed paper between the cake layers, wrap, seal and label. The cake can also be frozen complete except for the chocolate triangles, in which case, open freeze first then pack.

If you are making the cake and the chocolate triangles at separate times, it may be easier to use 20 ml/1 tablespoon of Bournville cocoa dissolved in a very little boiling water, instead of melted chocolate. The marbled pattern will vary on the cakes so choose the most attractive to use on top.

Harriet Hedgehog (see page 29); Lucy Ladybird (see page 28)

Lucy Ladybird

Illustrated on page 27

Metric		Imperial
175 g	**margarine**	6 oz
175 g	**caster sugar**	6 oz
3	**eggs**	3
150 g	**self-raising flour**	5 oz
5 ml	**baking powder**	1 teaspoon
25 g	**Bournville cocoa**	1 oz
	Decoration	
50 g	**desiccated coconut**	2 oz
80 ml	**water**	4 tablespoons
	red food colouring	
100 g	**butter**	4 oz
175 g	**icing sugar, sieved**	6 oz
30 ml	**Bournville cocoa**	1 tablespoon
about 23 cm	**thin strip of liquorice**	about 9 in
1	**packet Cadbury's Buttons**	1
2	**currants**	2

1.2-litre	**ovenproof basin, greased**	2-pint

The cake can be frozen complete if wrapped carefully, ideally in a large polythene rigid container. Otherwise, wrap in foil or a large polythene bag, seal, label and freeze. Allow about 4 hours at room temperature for the cake to thaw.

Choose a wide bowl so that the ladybird will turn out nice and round. Rub the Buttons in your hands before sticking them on to the cake.

Cream the margarine and sugar together really well. Gradually beat in the eggs with a spoonful of the flour. Sieve the flour, baking powder and cocoa together and fold in. Add a little milk if the mixture is too dry. Turn into the prepared basin and bake in a moderate oven (180°C, 350°F, Gas Mark 4) for about 1 hour. Test with a warm skewer to see that the cake is cooked in the centre. Leave in the basin to cool then turn out.

Mix the coconut with the water and stir in some bright red colouring to make it really red. Spread the coconut on a baking tray and dry in a slow oven (140°C, 275°F, Gas Mark 1) for about 1 hour. A warm airing cupboard would also be suitable but it will take a little longer.

To make the butter icing, cream the butter with the sieved icing sugar. Blend the cocoa with a little boiling water and stir into the icing. Spread icing over the flat, top side of the cake. Cut the cake in half down the middle and press the two iced surfaces together, making a mound. Lift the cake on to a flat plate or a cake board. Cover the cake with the remaining butter icing. Shape one end slightly more into a point for the 'head'. Press the dry, red coconut on to most of the cake, leaving the front area clear. Mark a line with a skewer as a guide. Split part of the liquorice and make a 'V' on the top then continue the line down the middle of the back. Mark lines on the face with liquorice too (as illustrated). Stick Buttons at intervals on to the coconut to make the 'spots'. Arrange two Buttons in position for the 'eyes' and stick the currants in the centre. The ladybird is now complete.

Birthday candles and holders can be stuck into the cake along the top, or extra butter icing can be piped round the base for them.

Harriet Hedgehog

Illustrated on page 27

Open freeze the complete cake. Wrap in foil then in polythene; label and seal. Allow at least 4 hours for the cake to thaw at room temperature.

Metric		Imperial
1 quantity	**cake mixture for Lucy Ladybird**	1 quantity
	(see page 28), made in the	
	same size bowl	
	Decoration	
100 g	**butter**	4 oz
175 g	**icing sugar, sieved**	6 oz
30 ml	**Bournville cocoa**	1 good tablespoon
2	**large packets Cadbury's Buttons**	2
1	**glacé cherry**	1
2	**roasted coffee beans or**	2
	seedless raisins	

Have the chocolate cake ready. Make the icing by beating the butter with the sieved icing sugar. Dissolve the cocoa in a very little boiling water and mix into the butter icing.

Spread the flat, top side of the cake with butter icing then cut it in half down the middle. Sandwich the two ends covered with icing together. Spread butter icing all over the cake and lift it on to a plate or cake board. Put a little extra icing at one end and form this into a point for the 'snout'. Cut each Button in half and stick them into the butter icing at an angle, covering all the cake except the front quarter. Make the points go in the same direction as they represent 'spines'. Mark the 'face' with a fork and put the cherry on the end, with the coffee beans or raisins in position for the 'eyes'.

Holiday Layer Cake

Illustrated opposite

Metric		Imperial
100 g	**Bournville plain chocolate**	4 oz
60 ml	**boiling water**	3 tablespoons
175 g	**self-raising flour**	7 oz
25 g	**Bournville cocoa**	1 oz
150 g	**butter**	6 oz
150 g	**caster sugar**	6 oz
5 ml	**vanilla essence**	1 teaspoon
4 size 2	**eggs, separated**	4 large
	little milk	
	Fudge Icing	
200 g	**Bournville plain chocolate**	8 oz
1	**small can evaporated milk**	1
225 g	**icing sugar, sieved**	8 oz
2 21.5-cm	**shallow cake tins, greased and base lined**	2 8½-inch

Open freeze the completed cake and when hard, wrap, seal and label.

This cake keeps exceptionally well in an airtight tin. The icing can be made separately well in advance then kept until required. It will harden but is easy to soften in a basin over a pan of hot water.

Break up the chocolate and put it into a small bowl with the hot water. Stir until melted and smooth. Sieve the flour and cocoa together. Cream the butter then beat in the sugar and the vanilla essence. Add the soft chocolate then the egg yolks. Fold in the dry ingredients with just enough milk to make a smooth consistency. Whisk the egg whites until stiff then fold them lightly into the cake mixture, making sure no large patches of white remain. Divide the mixture between the prepared tins. Bake in a moderate oven (180°C, 350°F, Gas Mark 4) for 25–30 minutes. Turn out and cool on a wire tray.

To make the icing, break up the chocolate and place it in a fairly large bowl over a pan of hot water. When the chocolate is completely melted, add the evaporated milk and beat the mixture together whilst still over the heat. Take the bowl off the heat and allow the mixture to cool a little before stirring in the sieved icing sugar. Put the bowl of icing into the refrigerator or stand in a bowl of cold water to speed up the setting. When it is hard enough, sandwich the cakes together with about one-third of the icing and spread the rest over the cake. Dab with a knife to form peaks. Lift the cake on to a plate.

Chip Cake (see page 34); Crusted Marble Cake (see page 24); Holiday Layer Cake (see above)

Intriguing Peppermint Cake

Metric		Imperial
5 size 2	**eggs**	5 large
125 g	**caster sugar**	5 oz
125 g	**plain flour**	5 oz
5 ml	**baking powder**	1 teaspoon
	pinch of salt	
2.5 ml	**peppermint essence**	$\frac{1}{2}$ teaspoon
about 1.25 ml	**green food colouring**	about $\frac{1}{4}$ teaspoon
20 ml	**Bournville cocoa**	1 tablespoon
	Decoration	
175 g	**butter**	6 oz
350 g	**icing sugar, sieved**	12 oz
45 ml	**Bournville cocoa**	3 tablespoons
40 g	**Bournville plain chocolate, grated**	$1\frac{1}{2}$ oz
35-cm × 25-cm	**Swiss roll tin, greased and lined**	14-inch × 10-inch
19–20-cm	**round cake tin, greased and base lined**	$7\frac{1}{2}$–8-inch
	greaseproof paper piping bag	

Freeze the complete cake. Pack, label and seal.

Although this cake may sound a little complicated to make, the effect is well worth the effort. Soft peppermint creams can be crushed and added to the butter icing in the centre.

Whisk the eggs and sugar together in a large bowl over a pan of hot water, or use an electric mixer as this is quite a big amount. Continue until the whisk will leave a very definite trail. Sieve the flour and baking powder with a pinch of salt then fold it carefully into the mixture, using a metal spoon, with a sharp cutting action. Make sure there are no pockets of flour left. Divide the mixture in half. To one half, add the peppermint essence and enough green food colouring to make the cake an attractive pale green. Turn this into the prepared Swiss roll tin and shake the tin to level the surface. Sieve the cocoa, fold into the remaining mixture and turn into the round tin. Bake the cakes, one above the other if necessary, in a fairly hot oven (200°C, 400°F, Gas Mark 6) for 12–15 minutes until springy when touched. The underneath cake may take a little longer than the one on top. Turn out on to wire trays to cool, removing the paper carefully.

Make up the butter icing by creaming the butter well then beating in the sieved icing sugar. Dissolve the cocoa in a little boiling water. Keep out a good spoonful of the plain butter icing then blend the cocoa into the remainder.

Cut the rectangular plain cake into five long even strips. Slice the chocolate cake horizontally through the centre, making two circles the same depth. Spread both of these with chocolate butter icing. Gently spread the cake strips too.

Place one of the chocolate circles flat on the table. On top of it, make a spiral with the plain cake strips, working from the centre outwards, joining all the strips together so that they are all used up. When it is completed, press the second chocolate cake circle on top, with the butter icing underneath. Cover the top and sides with the remaining chocolate butter icing in the usual way. Coat the sides with grated chocolate and lift the cake on to a plate.

Soften the reserved plain butter icing with a little hot water and blend in a few drops of the green food colouring. Fill the paper piping bag, cut the tip off the end and pipe straight lines on top of the cake, about 2.5 cm/1 inch apart. Draw a skewer in alternate directions across the lines, again evenly spaced, making a feather pattern. Any extra green icing can be used round the edge or kept for another occasion.

No Bake Fudge Slice

Illustrated on page 51

Wrap, seal, label and freeze the slice complete. Use within 3 months.

Metric		Imperial
100 g	**butter**	4 oz
40 ml	**golden syrup**	2 tablespoons
200 g	**sweet biscuits**	8 oz
25 g	**seedless raisins**	1 oz
50 g	**glacé cherries, quartered**	2 oz
125 g	**Bournville plain chocolate, chopped**	5 oz
	Fudge Icing	
50 g	**Bournville plain chocolate**	2 oz
40 ml	**water**	2 tablespoons
25 g	**butter**	1 oz
150 g	**icing sugar, sieved**	6 oz
0.5-kg	**loaf tin, greased with butter and base lined**	1-lb

Melt the butter and syrup in a saucepan. Crush the biscuits but do not make them too fine. Add the biscuits, raisins, quartered cherries and chopped chocolate. Stir the ingredients together then press them firmly into the tin. Leave overnight to harden. Later turn out on to a board.

To make the icing, break the chocolate into squares and melt in a pan with the water and butter. Heat gently until completely liquid. Off the heat, beat in the sieved icing sugar, beating until the icing is smooth and thick. Spread the icing over the cake then dust with icing sugar.

Chip Cake

Illustrated on page 31

Metric		Imperial
275 g	**plain flour**	10 oz
5 ml	**baking powder**	1 teaspoon
175 g	**butter**	6 oz
225 g	**caster sugar**	8 oz
4 size 2	**eggs**	4 large
	grated rind of 1 orange	
50 g	**Bournville plain chocolate**	2 oz
	Icing	
100 g	**Bournville plain chocolate**	4 oz
45 ml	**water**	3 tablespoons
5 ml	**flavourless salad oil**	1 teaspoon
25 g	**caster sugar**	1 oz
	Decoration	
	3 orange jelly slices	
18-cm	**round deep cake tin,**	7-inch
	greased and base lined	

Freeze the cake without the icing. Wrap, label and seal. The icing may be put on to the cake as soon as it comes out of the freezer.

This is a plain cake which keeps well. The mixture is fairly dry and if a slightly softer texture is preferred, the juice of up to half an orange may be added before the flour.

Sieve the flour and baking powder together. Cream the butter and sugar together. Add the eggs one at a time, with a little of the sieved dry ingredients if the mixture shows any sign of curdling. Fold in the remaining dry ingredients and the orange rind. Chop the chocolate into small pieces and stir into the mixture. Place in the prepared tin, hollowing out the centre slightly. Bake in a moderate oven (180°C, 350°F, Gas Mark 4) for 1–1¼ hours. Test with a warm skewer to see that the cake is cooked through in the centre. Lift out on to a wire tray to cool. Peel off the paper.

To make the icing, break the chocolate into a pan. Measure in the water, oil and sugar. Melt the chocolate over a gentle heat, stirring occasionally to blend all the ingredients. Leave the icing to cool and thicken enough to coat the back of a wooden spoon before pouring it over the cake, still on the wire tray. Allow the icing to dribble down the sides. Cut the jelly slices in half and arrange on top. Later when the icing has set, transfer the cake to a plate.

*Party Candles (see page 38);
Yule Log (see page 36);
Shaggy Dog Cake (see
page 36)*

Yule Log

Illustrated on page 35

Metric		Imperial
	icing sugar	
350 g	**chocolate butter icing**	12 oz
	(1½ quantities, see page 14)	
2	**chocolate Swiss rolls, filled (see page 86)**	2
28-cm	**square cake board**	11-inch
	Christmas cake decorations	

Cover the cake board with sieved icing sugar. Spread butter icing over both the Swiss rolls. Put one on the board. Cut a slice off one end of the second Swiss roll then another third, cut at an angle. Stick the pieces on as 'branches', with the icing, covering all the ends. Place the slice on the top of the roll. Form lines in the icing to give the log texture. Arrange Christmas trees, robins and any other decorations in position. Dust with icing sugar.

Open freeze the Yule Log. Wrap carefully in foil when the cake is hard. Allow a minimum of 3 hours for the cake to defrost.

Shaggy Dog Cake

Illustrated on page 35

Metric		Imperial
125 g	**butter**	5 oz
225 g	**icing sugar, sieved**	8 oz
25 g	**Bournville cocoa**	1 oz
1	**chocolate Swiss roll, filled (see page 86)**	1
	Decoration	
2	**Cadbury's Buttons**	2
1	**glacé cherry**	1
1	**chocolate finger biscuit**	1

Cream the butter with the sieved icing sugar. Dissolve the cocoa in a little boiling water and beat into the butter icing.

Cover the Swiss roll with the butter icing, including the ends, then stick it on to a rectangular cake board or dish. Fill in the gap at the bottom of the Swiss roll too. Mark lines with a fork from the top down to the bottom of the Swiss roll, in the butter icing, flicking up the ends to make the shaggy coat. Stick the Buttons on at one end for the 'eyes', with a blob of icing in the centre of each. Place a cherry in position for the 'nose' and the biscuit standing up at the other end, for the 'tail'. This cake makes a simple and popular birthday cake.

Open freeze the cake without the biscuit tail. Later pack carefully, seal and label. Allow about 3 hours at room temperature for the cake to thaw.

A small cake can be stuck on the front of the Swiss roll to make a separate head. This is useful when you require a slightly bigger cake.

INDIVIDUAL CAKES

For many women their cooking skills are not complete unless they can produce an attractive display of small cakes for the tea table. Many ideas stem from one basic cake method, with decorations made to suit the occasion. As iced cakes generally keep better than plain ones and individual cakes are less trouble to serve than large cakes, it is no wonder they are so popular for more formal receptions.

Again we have included some special novelty ideas for the children which they could help to make. But sophisticated tastes are not forgotten—spiced with cinnamon, the Cream Puffs literally melt in the mouth.

Fancy Cakes

Illustrated on page 39

Metric		Imperial
100 g	**soft margarine or butter**	4 oz
100 g	**caster sugar**	4 oz
2	**eggs**	2
100 g	**self-raising flour, sieved**	4 oz
20 ml	**Bournville cocoa, sieved**	1 tablespoon
20	**paper cake cases**	20

Cream the margarine and the sugar until lighter in colour and texture. Gradually beat in the eggs and fold in the sieved flour with the cocoa. Add a little milk if necessary to make a soft dropping consistency. Place the paper cases close together on a baking tray, or put the cases into a tray of bun tins. Fill with mixture and bake in a moderate oven (180°C, 350°F, Gas Mark 4) for 12–15 minutes. Cool on a wire tray.

Makes 20

Top Hats

Make up a batch of Fancy Cakes. With a small plain pastry cutter measuring about 2 cm/1 inch, cut out the centre but do not cut right through the cakes. Fill the centres with a whirl of the economical vanilla icing. Replace the centre piece of cake and dust with icing sugar.

Economical Vanilla Icing

Beat 75 g/3 oz soft margarine with 225 g/8 oz sieved icing sugar and 45 ml/3 tablespoons milk until it is light in colour and texture. Add 2.5 ml/½ teaspoon vanilla essence and any food colouring that may be needed.

To make chocolate icing: dissolve 25 g/1 oz Bournville cocoa in a little boiling water and stir into the icing.

Decorated Cakes

Make a variety of designs by piping vanilla or chocolate icing on the small cakes. Decorate with Cadbury's Buttons, Flake and some softened jam. Cherries, nuts and angelica are also colourful additions. Grated Bournville plain chocolate over vanilla icing makes a simple decoration. The small cakes may also be feather iced, made in the same way as the Feather Iced Cake (page 17).

For Madeleines, see Owl Madeleines, page 46.

Party Candles

Illustrated on page 35

Metric		Imperial
1	**chocolate Swiss roll**	1
8	**small Cadbury's Flakes**	8
312-g	**can mandarin oranges**	11-oz
about 50 g	**vanilla butter icing (see page 14)**	about 2 oz
2	**glacé cherries**	2

greaseproof paper piping bag

Cut the Swiss roll into 8 even slices. Stand a Flake in the centre of each, sticking it through the cake. Drain the juice from the mandarin oranges. Arrange the mandarin segments on the slices of Swiss roll, round the Flake. Fill a paper piping bag with the butter icing, cut off the tip and pipe dribbles of the icing coming down from the top of each Flake. Cut the cherries into four and stand one piece upright on the top of each Flake, to represent the candle 'flame'.

Makes 8

Peach slices are equally effective on the candles. White glacé icing (see page 14) may be used instead of the butter icing but it should be quite thick so that it does not run off.

Fancy Cakes (see page 37); Marzipan Log Cakes (see page 40)

Marzipan Log Cakes

Illustrated on page 39

Metric		Imperial
100 g	**butter**	4 oz
100 g	**caster sugar**	4 oz
2	**eggs**	2
100 g	**self-raising flour, sieved**	4 oz
80 ml	**apricot jam**	4 tablespoons
225 g	**marzipan**	8 oz
	red and green food colouring	
5 ml	**Bournville cocoa**	1 teaspoon
	Icing	
200 g	**Bournville plain chocolate**	8 oz
25 g	**slightly salted butter**	1 oz
45 ml	**water**	3 tablespoons
50 g	**icing sugar**	2 oz
18-cm	**square cake tin, greased and base lined**	7-inch

Cream the butter and sugar together until quite soft. Add the eggs then fold in the sieved flour. Turn into the prepared tin and bake in a moderately hot oven (190°C, 375°F, Gas Mark 5) for about 20 minutes. Turn out and cool on a wire tray.

Trim the cake edges and split the cake in half. Spread the cake with jam and sandwich together again. Spread the jam thinly over the top. Cut the cake in half.

Divide the marzipan into three. Work a few drops of red colouring into one amount, green colouring into another and the cocoa into the third amount, kneading it well so that the colours are thoroughly blended. Divide each colour into two then form into six rolls the same length as the cake strips. Lay two rolls together along the centre of each cake strip, with one on the top, making a triangle. Lift the pieces of cake on to a wire tray.

Melt the chocolate with the butter and water in a small saucepan and stir gently until melted. Beat in the icing sugar off the heat. Carefully spoon this icing over the cake strips and marzipan. Spread the sides with the icing too. It is a little difficult to get the texture smooth but when the cakes are completely covered, shake the wire tray slightly to level the icing. Leave to set. Later cut each cake strip diagonally into about 4 slices, with a piece at either end.

Makes 8 slices

Continental Cases

Metric		Imperial
6–8	**individual meringue cases**	6–8
125 g	**Bournville plain chocolate**	5 oz
40 g	**unsalted butter**	1½ oz
125 ml	**single cream**	¼ pint
40 ml	**rum**	2 tablespoons
50 g	**glacé cherries**	2 oz
50 g	**cake crumbs**	2 oz
35 ml	**apricot jam**	1 heaped tablespoon

Glacé cherries are sometimes very sticky. Wash them in warm water to remove the syrup, using a sieve, then dry in an airy place, on kitchen paper.

piping bag and star vegetable pipe

Have the meringue cases ready. Break the chocolate into a pan and melt it with the butter and cream. Take the pan off the heat and beat the mixture quite hard until it thickens. Add half the rum and leave to cool.

Keep 3 or 4 of the cherries aside for the decoration and chop the remainder. Stir them into the cake crumbs and bind the mixture together with the jam and remaining rum. Divide the filling between the meringue cases. Fill the piping bag with the chocolate mixture and pipe a large whirl on top of each meringue case. Decorate with half a glacé cherry.

Makes 6–8

Krackolates

Metric		Imperial
50 g	**butter or margarine**	2 oz
25 ml	**Cadbury's drinking chocolate**	2 tablespoons
40 ml	**golden syrup**	2 tablespoons
75 g	**cornflakes**	3 oz

baking tray, greased

Melt the butter in a fairly large pan with the drinking chocolate and syrup. Stir continuously and bring to the boil, making a thin sauce. Stir in the cornflakes, making quite sure they are completely covered. Leave the mixture in the pan for about 20 minutes to cool so that it becomes sticky. Spoon the mixture into heaps on a greased baking tray and leave until they cool completely and set quite hard. The mixture may also be placed straight into paper cake cases.

Makes 12

Cream Puffs

Illustrated opposite

Metric		Imperial
1 quantity	**choux pastry (see page 80)**	1 quantity
75 g	**Bournville plain chocolate**	3 oz
60 ml	**water**	3 tablespoons
1	**egg yolk**	1
125 ml	**double cream**	¼ pint
	good pinch of ground cinnamon	
25 g	**icing sugar, sieved**	1 oz
	Decoration	
	little icing sugar	

piping bag and star vegetable pipe

Make up the choux pastry as described. Place the mixture into the piping bag. Grease a baking tray then dust it with flour, shaking off any excess. Pipe 4 large stars on the tray, using half the mixture. Space them well apart as they will rise and puff out. Bake in a moderate oven (180°C, 350°F, Gas Mark 4) for 10 minutes then increase the heat to moderately hot (190°C, 375°F, Gas Mark 5) for another 10 minutes. Now increase the heat again to fairly hot (200°C, 400°F, Gas Mark 6) for about 20 minutes until the puffs are golden brown and crisp on the base. Cool on a wire tray, making a slit in the side with a knife to let the steam escape. Make a second batch in the same way.

Break the chocolate into a small pan. Add the water and egg yolk. Stir over a low heat until the chocolate has completely melted and the mixture thickens. Cool completely. Whip the cream, cinnamon and sieved icing sugar together until it will hold its shape nicely. Fold the cold chocolate into the cream. Divide the cream filling between the puffs, using a piping bag if it is more convenient. Dust with icing sugar.

Makes 8

Open freeze the completed puffs. Later, wrap, label and seal. Use within 3 months.

There are several methods for cooking choux pastry but we have found a rising temperature to be consistently the most successful.

Coconut Heaps (see page 44);
Cream Puffs (see above)

Coconut Heaps

Illustrated on page 43

Metric		Imperial
2	**egg whites**	2
100 g	**caster sugar**	4 oz
50 g	**Cadbury's drinking chocolate, sieved**	2 oz
125 g	**desiccated coconut**	5 oz
	about 5 glacé cherries	
2	**baking trays**	2
	rice paper or Bakewell paper	

Rice paper can be eaten. This is a lighter mixture than the more traditional coconut pyramids.

Prepare the trays first by covering them with the rice paper or Bakewell paper cut to fit. Whisk the egg whites until really stiff. Add the sugar and whisk again until the mixture is stiff again and thick. Stir in the sieved drinking chocolate and the coconut. Drop spoonsful of mixture on to the baking trays, making at least 10. Stick half a cherry on top of each. Bake in a slow oven (150°C, 300°F, Gas Mark 2) for about 45 minutes. Lift them off the Bakewell paper or peel off any excess rice paper and cool.

Makes 10

Chocolate Sponge Fingers

Illustrated on page 119

Metric		Imperial
2 size 2	**eggs**	2 large
50 g	**caster sugar**	2 oz
50 g	**plain flour, sieved**	2 oz
15 ml	**Bournville cocoa**	1 tablespoon
	sponge finger tins	

These fingers freeze well. Pack, label and freeze.

The sponge fingers can be sandwiched together with whipped cream, butter icing (see page 14) or jam. For a special treat, melt about 100 g/ 4 oz Bournville plain chocolate and dip both ends of the sponge fingers into it.

Whisk the eggs and the sugar in a fairly large bowl over a pan of hot water, or use an electric hand beater. Continue whisking until the mixture will leave a very definite trail. Fold in the sieved flour with the cocoa and 15 ml/1 tablespoon of warm water. Spoon the mixture into the greased sponge finger tins. There will be about 20. The cooking time is fairly quick so the mixture will keep to cook a second batch. Bake in a fairly hot oven (200°C, 400°F, Gas Mark 6) for 10–12 minutes. Turn out and cool on a wire tray.

Makes 20–24

Strawberry Chocolate Boxes

Metric		Imperial
200 g	**Bournville plain chocolate**	8 oz
100 g	**soft margarine**	4 oz
100 g	**caster sugar**	4 oz
2	**eggs**	2
100 g	**self-raising flour, sieved**	4 oz
100 g	**granulated sugar**	4 oz
125 ml	**water**	$\frac{1}{4}$ pint
20 ml	**curaçao or orange juice**	1 tablespoon
60–80 ml	**strawberry jam**	3–4 tablespoons
90 ml	**double cream**	6 tablespoons
12	**fresh strawberries**	12
12	**chocolate leaves (see page 10)**	12
28-cm × 18-cm	**Swiss roll tin, greased and base lined**	11-inch × 7-inch

Melt the chocolate in a bowl placed over a pan of hot water. Have a large piece of waxed paper ready and spread the chocolate on to it, forming a rectangle measuring 31 cm × 23 cm/12 inches × 9 inches. Leave to set.

Measure the margarine and sugar into a bowl. Add the eggs and sieved flour. Beat the mixture together for a good 2 minutes so that it is well blended. Spread in the prepared tin and bake the cake in a moderately hot oven (190°C, 375°F, Gas Mark 5), for about 20 minutes. Turn out on to a wire tray to cool.

Dissolve the granulated sugar with the water in a saucepan, over gentle heat. When the sugar granules have completely disappeared and the liquid is clear, bring the syrup to the boil. Cook rapidly for a minute. Add the curaçao or orange juice off the heat. Cool the syrup a little.

Slice the cake through the centre. Spread one piece with jam and sandwich the cake together again. Trim the edges. Pour over the syrup and leave it to soak through. Cut the cake into 12 squares, measuring 3.5 cm/1$\frac{1}{2}$ inches. Melt a little more jam and brush it over the sides of the cake squares. Cut the chocolate into the same sized squares, using a sharp knife. Press one on to each side of each cake. Whip the cream and pipe a whirl on top or put it on with a spoon. Make sure the strawberries are clean then place one on each of the cakes, with a chocolate leaf sticking out at an angle. Arrange the cakes on a plate.

Makes 12

Owl Madeleines

Illustrated opposite

Metric		Imperial
25 g	**Bournville cocoa**	1 OZ
100 g	**self-raising flour**	4 OZ
	pinch of salt	
2	**eggs**	2
100 g	**soft margarine**	4 OZ
100 g	**caster sugar**	4 OZ
	Decoration	
about 60 ml	**apricot jam**	about 3 tablespoons
40 ml	**water**	2 tablespoons
50 g	**desiccated coconut**	2 OZ
	little plain or chocolate butter icing or	
	glacé icing (see page 14)	
1	**large packet Cadbury's Buttons**	1
4	**glacé cherries**	4

dariole moulds, greased

The cakes may be frozen complete but the Buttons and cherry may need sticking on again when the cakes are thawed. Open freeze then pack, label and seal.

The easiest way to coat these cakes is to stick each one on a skewer before covering with jam and coconut.

Sieve the cocoa, flour and salt into a bowl. Add the eggs, margarine and sugar. Beat the ingredients together, making the cake by the one-stage method. When quite smooth, spoon enough mixture into the moulds to come halfway up. There will be enough for between 12 and 15 cakes, depending on the size of the dariole moulds. Bake the cakes in batches if necessary. Place on a baking tray and bake in a moderately hot oven (190°C, 375°F, Gas Mark 5) for about 20 minutes. Test with a warm skewer to see if they are cooked through. Shake out on to a wire tray and bake the next batch, removing any cake crumbs that may be left in the moulds.

Melt the jam with the water. Coat each cake with jam then roll in the coconut. Stick two Buttons on each cake with the icing, for the 'eyes', with a spot in the centre of each. Complete the 'owls' with a piece of cherry sticking out as the 'beak'. The cakes can be placed in paper cake cases if wished.

Makes about 15

Madeleines: Follow the above recipe but omit the Buttons and add a whirl of cream on top with a cherry.

Fir Cone Cakes (see page 48);
Owl Madeleines (see above);
Merry Mice (see page 49)

Fir Cone Cakes

Illustrated on page 47

Metric		Imperial
20 ml	**Bournville cocoa**	1 tablespoon
50 g	**self-raising flour**	2 oz
	pinch of salt	
50 g	**soft margarine**	2 oz
50 g	**caster sugar**	2 oz
1	**egg**	1
	Butter icing	
50 g	**butter**	2 oz
100 g	**icing sugar, sieved**	4 oz
20 ml	**Bournville cocoa**	1 tablespoon
20 ml	**boiling water**	1 tablespoon
	vanilla essence	
	Decoration	
2	**large packets Cadbury's Buttons**	2
10	**bun tins, greased**	10

Open freeze the cakes covered with the butter icing but omit the Buttons as they come off easily in the freezer. Wrap, seal and label the cakes. Use within 3 months. Cover with Buttons when the cakes are thawed.

The number of buns will vary according to the size of your tins.

Sieve the cocoa and flour with a pinch of salt into a bowl. Add the margarine, sugar and egg then beat thoroughly until well mixed. Divide mixture between the tins, shaking each one so that the mixture settles. Bake in a moderately hot oven (190°C, 375°F, Gas Mark 5) for 15–20 minutes. Turn out and cool on a wire tray.

Make the butter icing by creaming the butter with the sieved icing sugar. Mix the cocoa with the boiling water then add to the butter icing with a few drops of vanilla essence. Mix well. Turn the buns upside down and cover the tops and sides with butter icing.

Divide the Buttons evenly between the cakes; polish them in the palm of your hand and arrange in overlapping rows. A small piece of fir may be stuck into one end of each cake.

Makes 10

Merry Mice

Illustrated on page 47

Metric		Imperial
20 ml	**Bournville cocoa**	1 tablespoon
50 g	**self-raising flour**	2 oz
50 g	**soft margarine**	2 oz
50 g	**caster sugar**	2 oz
1	**egg**	1
	Icing	
100 g	**Bournville plain chocolate**	4 oz
45 ml	**water**	3 tablespoons
5 ml	**flavourless salad oil**	1 teaspoon
25 g	**caster sugar**	1 oz
	Decoration	
10	**marshmallows**	10
1	**large packet Cadbury's Buttons**	1
50 g	**vanilla butter icing (see page 14)**	2 oz
	glacé cherries and currants	
about 5 cm long	**angelica strips**	about 2 inches long
	thin strips of liquorice	
10	**paper cake cases**	10
10	**bun tins**	10

Sieve the cocoa and flour into a bowl. Add the margarine, sugar and the egg. Beat the mixture together until thoroughly blended. Put the paper cases into the bun tins and divide the mixture between them. Place on a baking tray. Bake in a moderately hot oven (190°C, 375°F, Gas Mark 5) for 15–20 minutes until springy to the touch and cooked. Leave to cool.

Break up the chocolate and melt in a small pan, with the water, oil and sugar. Stir gently until melted. It should be a really glossy icing. Press a marshmallow on to each cake. Cool the icing slightly then spoon it over the top of the cakes. Leave the icing to set. With a hot, sharp knife, make two slits at either side of the marshmallow and press Buttons into these for the 'ears'. Pipe two small stars of butter icing in the centre for the 'eyes' and stick a currant on. Pipe another star of icing for the 'mouth', with a quarter of a cherry on top. Stick thin strips of angelica in at either side for the 'whiskers'. Finally, use a skewer to make a hole in the back in which to stick a liquorice 'tail'. Complete all the cakes in the same way.

Makes 10

Popper Bars

Illustrated opposite

Metric		Imperial
25 g	**butter**	1 oz
20 ml	**golden syrup**	1 tablespoon
20 ml	**sugar**	1 tablespoon
20 ml	**Bournville cocoa**	1 tablespoon
25 g	**'Puffed Wheat'**	1 oz
10	**Cadbury's Flakes**	10
10	**paper cake cases**	10

Experiment with other types of cereal mixed into the cocoa mixture. This is an easy recipe for children to make.

Put the butter, syrup, sugar and cocoa into a fairly large pan then stir over a gentle heat to melt. Stir in the 'Puffed Wheat' off the heat. Place one Flake into each paper case, flattening the paper slightly. Divide the mixture between the Flakes and press it on the centre, sticking it all together. Leave to set which will only take a short time.

Makes 10

Munchies

Illustrated opposite

Metric		Imperial
100 g	**butter**	4 oz
80 ml	**golden syrup**	4 tablespoons
40 ml	**Bournville cocoa**	2 tablespoons
200 g	**Swiss style breakfast cereal**	8 oz
16	**small paper cake cases**	16

Children will enjoy making this recipe as it is very easy to do. The best way to accurately measure golden syrup is to heat a metal spoon, or a metal scale pan if larger amounts are required. The syrup then slides off the spoon easily.

Melt the butter and syrup in a good sized pan with the cocoa and when it is dissolved, bring to the boil. Take it off the heat and stir in the cereal. Press the mixture into a round spoon, or use a small ice cream scoop and make heaps. Arrange these in the paper cases and leave in the refrigerator for a couple of hours.

Makes 12–16

No Bake Fudge Slice (see page 33); Popper Bars (see above); Munchies (see above)

BISCUITS AND BAKES

There are comparatively few people who are not called upon at one time or another to give produce for a local market or fund-raising activity. What better than biscuits, cookies and bakes that can be made quite easily and relatively cheaply? Home-made biscuits look and smell particularly appetising. There are recipes for all kinds, both cooked and uncooked. Plain, iced, blends of fruit and spice, novelty ideas to ring the changes.

Many of the goodies can be packed in the food freezer ready for use at a moment's notice—that is if there are any left after the scrumptious smells have wafted out from the kitchen. Make some to keep in the biscuit tin too, for nibbling on the many occasions when we all want a biscuit.

Swiss Circles

Illustrated on page 55

Metric		Imperial
150 g	**butter**	6 oz
25 g	**icing sugar, sieved**	1 oz
100 g	**self-raising flour**	4 oz
25 g	**cornflour**	1 oz
25 g	**Cadbury's drinking chocolate**	1 oz
	few drops of vanilla essence	
2	**baking trays, greased**	2
	piping bag and star pipe	

Cream the butter with the sieved icing sugar until light in colour. Sieve the flour, cornflour and drinking chocolate together. Beat them in gradually, making sure there are no pockets of flour left. Beat in the essence and continue to beat until the mixture is soft enough to pipe. Fill the piping bag then pipe circles on to the trays, spacing them apart as the mixture will spread. Bake in a hot oven (220°C, 425°F, Gas Mark 7) for 6 minutes then lower the heat to moderate (180°C, 350°F, Gas Mark 4) for about a further 6 minutes, until the biscuits are cooked. Cool before carefully lifting from the tray. The mixture is very short so has to be handled carefully.

Makes 10

The biscuits will freeze but should be packed very carefully in a rigid container as they break easily. Wrap, seal and label. Keep up to 2 months.

25 g/1 oz extra flour may be added if the mixture is too short for your liking. The biscuits can be finished off with half a glacé cherry on the join, or sprinkled with flaked almonds, added before baking.

Farmhouse Biscuits

Metric		Imperial
50 g	lard	2 oz
50 g	soft margarine	2 oz
75 g	caster sugar	3 oz
20 ml	Bournville cocoa	1 tablespoon
125 g	self-raising flour	5 oz
75 g	porridge oats	3 oz
2.5 ml	vanilla essence	$\frac{1}{2}$ teaspoon
2	baking trays, greased	2

Pack in a rigid container, seal and label before freezing.

It does not really matter if these biscuits are uneven in size. If you want to be particularly accurate, form the dough into a roll and cut it into 24 even-sized pieces. Roll these into balls and proceed.

Beat the lard and margarine together, then beat in the sugar. Sieve the cocoa and flour into the mixture. Mix it all together with the oats and vanilla essence. If it is too crumbly, knead the mixture by hand. Roll small amounts of the dough into balls between the palms of your hands. Arrange them on the baking trays and flatten each one with a fork. Do not make them too thin. There will be enough for two trays so either alternate the trays in the oven halfway through cooking time or bake them in batches. The biscuits do not spread much. Bake in a slow oven (150°C, 300°F, Gas Mark 2) for about 35 minutes. Lift off and cool on a wire tray.

Makes 24

No Bake Squares

Metric		Imperial
150 g	mixed digestive and sweet biscuits	6 oz
50 g	hazelnuts	2 oz
50 g	seedless raisins	2 oz
50 g	Bournville plain chocolate	2 oz
30 ml	golden syrup	2 tablespoons
75 g	butter	3 oz
19-cm	square tin, greased	7½-inch

The recipe varies each time it is made, depending on the kind of biscuit that is used. This is an ideal recipe to use up the bits in the bottom of the biscuit tin, or broken biscuits. Home-made ones can also be used.

Crush the biscuits but do not make them too fine. Chop the hazelnuts and add to the biscuits, with the raisins. Break up the chocolate and melt it with the syrup and butter. When it is quite smooth, stir the liquid into the biscuit crumbs and mix thoroughly. Press into the tin and leave to harden. Cut into squares.

Makes 16

Bourbon Dominoes

Illustrated opposite

Metric		Imperial
100 g	**butter or soft margarine**	4 oz
100 g	**caster sugar**	4 oz
1	**egg, beaten**	1
225 g	**plain flour**	9 oz
30 g	**Bournville cocoa**	1 oz
	pinch of salt	
	Butter icing	
75 g	**butter**	3 oz
150 g	**icing sugar, sieved**	6 oz
2.5 ml	**vanilla essence**	$\frac{1}{2}$ teaspoon
2	**baking trays, greased**	2

The dominoes can be frozen complete. Pack in a rigid container, seal and label.

When making the holes, twist the skewer round so that they become big enough for the butter icing to come through later.
For older tastes, make the butter icing coffee flavoured.

Cream the fat and sugar, and gradually add the beaten egg. Sieve in the flour and cocoa with a pinch of salt and blend the mixture together with a wooden spoon. Knead lightly in the bowl. Place the biscuit dough between 2 sheets of grease-proof paper to avoid marking it with flour and roll out to about 3-mm/$\frac{1}{8}$-inch thickness. Accurately mark rectangles with a ruler, measuring 3 cm × 7 cm/$1\frac{1}{4}$ inches × $2\frac{3}{4}$ inches; cut out and lift on to greased baking trays. Roll out the dough again as necessary. Make an even number of biscuits, there should be about 48. Mark a line across the centre with a skewer. Make holes in half the biscuits to represent the dominoe numbers and remember to have a double six to start the game. Leave the biscuits on their trays for about 30 minutes to relax, then bake in a moderate oven (180°C, 350°F, Gas Mark 4) for 10–15 minutes. It may be necessary to cook a second batch, or rotate the trays in the oven. Cool the biscuits on a wire tray.

To make the icing, soften the butter then beat the sieved icing sugar into it so that it becomes much lighter. 20 ml/1 tablespoon of hot water may be added if the butter icing is too stiff. Beat in the essence. Spread the underside of the plain biscuits quite thickly with butter icing and sandwich the others to them, pressing them together so that the icing comes through the holes. Scrape off any excess icing. The dominoes are now ready.

Makes about 24 biscuits

Island Slices (see page 58); Swiss Circles (see page 52); Bourbon Dominoes (see above); Crunchy Cookies (see page 56)

V·Good

Crunchy Cookies

Illustrated on page 55

Metric		Imperial
100 g	**margarine**	4 oz
100 g	**caster sugar**	4 oz
I	**egg, beaten**	I
2.5 ml	**vanilla essence**	½ teaspoon
100 g	**plain flour, sieved**	4 oz
2.5 ml	**bicarbonate of soda**	½ teaspoon
50 g	**Bournvita**	2 oz
50 g	**rolled oats**	2 oz
2	**baking trays, greased**	2

Beat the margarine and sugar together. Add the beaten egg and essence then the sieved flour and bicarbonate of soda. Finally stir in the Bournvita and rolled oats. Place teaspoonsful of mixture on greased baking trays, allowing room for them to spread. Bake in a moderately hot oven (190°C, 375°F, Gas Mark 5) for 10–12 minutes until browned nicely. Cool for a few minutes then lift on to a wire tray.

Makes about 32

These cookies freeze well. Place in a rigid container, seal and label.

For a special occasion, glacé icing (see page 14) can be zigzagged over the cookies, or perhaps piped as initials for children.

Chocolate Concrete

Illustrated on page 59

Metric		Imperial
75 g	**margarine**	3 oz
50 g	**white fat**	2 oz
50 g	**caster sugar**	2 oz
150 g	**plain flour**	6 oz
25 g	**Bournville cocoa**	I oz
50 g	**biscuit crumbs or**	2 oz
	browned breadcrumbs	
	Icing	
350 g	**icing sugar**	8-10 oz ~~12 oz~~
30 g	**Bournville cocoa**	½ oz ~~1 oz~~
20-cm × 30-cm	**Swiss roll tin, greased**	8-inch × 12-inch

Beat the fats together really well, then add the sugar. Sieve the flour with the cocoa and work into the mixture with the finely crushed biscuits or breadcrumbs. Spread evenly in the

Freeze the biscuits cut up in the tray, without the icing. Wrap, seal and label.

Do not be put off by the name, which is local to the Midlands. The biscuits are light in texture. They keep exceptionally well when kept in an airtight tin. Home-made breadcrumbs should be used for this recipe, or the broken biscuits from the biscuit tin.

tin, using a palette knife. Bake in a moderate oven (180°C, 350°F, Gas Mark 4) for 25 minutes. Cut up the biscuits straight away, making 24 pieces. Cool in the tin.

Sieve the icing sugar and cocoa into a bowl. Slowly mix in just enough water to make a spreading consistency. Pour all the icing on to the centre of the biscuits in the tray then with a palette knife, spread it over the surface. Do not lift up the knife at all. Carefully lift the biscuits on to a wire tray. When the icing has set, trim the edges with a sharp knife.

Makes 24 biscuits

Ginger Shorties

Illustrated on page 63

Freeze the squares for up to 3 months. Put waxed paper between the squares and pack carefully. Wrap, seal and label. Defrost at room temperature.

Do not use *soft* margarine in this recipe as the consistency becomes too soft with it.

Metric		Imperial
175 g	plain flour	6 oz
	pinch of salt	
100 g	butter	4 oz
50 g	caster sugar	2 oz
50 g	Bournville plain chocolate	2 oz
40 g	crystallised ginger	$1\frac{1}{2}$ oz
	Decoration	
	little caster sugar	
	Icing	
20 ml	Bournville cocoa	1 tablespoon
40 ml	boiling water	2 tablespoons
15 g	butter or margarine	$\frac{1}{2}$ oz
100 g	icing sugar, sieved	4 oz
5-cm	pastry cutter	2-inch
	baking tray	

Sieve the flour and salt together. Rub in the butter until the mixture resembles breadcrumbs. Stir in the sugar. Chop the chocolate and ginger into fairly small pieces and stir in. Knead the dough together, and on a lightly floured surface, roll out to 5 mm/$\frac{1}{4}$ inch thick. Cut out the biscuits with the cutter, rolling the dough again in between. Place the biscuits on a baking tray. Bake in a moderately hot oven (190°C, 375°F, Gas Mark 5) for 10–15 minutes until golden brown. Lift off the tray and dredge with caster sugar.

Sieve the cocoa and mix with the boiling water for the icing. Beat in the butter then the sieved icing sugar to make a smooth and shiny icing. Dip the biscuits into the icing, covering about one-third of the circle. Leave them to set.

Makes about 22

Island Slices

Illustrated on page 55

Metric		Imperial
100 g	**plain flour**	4 oz
10 ml	**Bournville cocoa**	2 teaspoons
	pinch of salt	
50 g	**butter**	2 oz
50 g	**caster sugar**	2 oz
1	**egg yolk**	1
	Filling	
50 g	**butter**	2 oz
1	**small can condensed milk**	1
60 ml	**icing sugar**	3 tablespoons
20 ml	**Bournville cocoa**	1 tablespoon
200 g	**desiccated coconut**	8 oz
	Icing	
125 g	**Cadbury's dairy milk chocolate**	4 oz

18-cm × 28-cm	**cake tin, about 2.5 cm/**	7-inch × 11-inch
	1-inch deep	

Sieve the flour and cocoa with a pinch of salt. Rub in the butter until the mixture resembles breadcrumbs, then add the sugar. Bind the mixture together with the egg yolk and a very little water if necessary. Roll out the pastry to fit the tin and line it carefully. Prick the base with a fork and bake the case blind in a moderate oven (180°C, 350°F, Gas Mark 4) for 15–20 minutes. Leave in the tin.

Melt the butter with the condensed milk in a saucepan. Sieve the icing sugar with the cocoa and mix into the saucepan with the coconut. Spread filling over the pastry base and leave it to get quite cold before spreading with chocolate.

Melt the chocolate carefully in a bowl over a pan of hot, not boiling water. Do not stir. Spread the chocolate over the filling, using a palette knife. Mark the top with a fork. When the chocolate is set, cut down the centre then into slices.

Makes 16

Freeze the slices before icing with chocolate, preferably whilst still in the tin. Wrap, seal and label. Defrost at room temperature. Cover with melted chocolate and cut into slices.

Melted Bournville plain chocolate may be substituted for the milk chocolate, if a stronger taste is preferred.

Chocolate Concrete (see page 56); Crackle Snaps (see page 60); Topsy Turvy Bars (see page 60); Peppermint Squares (see page 61); Frosted Malted Bars (see page 62)

Crackle Snaps

Illustrated on page 59

Metric		Imperial
75 g	**plain flour**	3 OZ
25 g	**caster sugar**	1 OZ
50 g	**butter**	2 OZ
	Topping	
25 g	**butter**	1 OZ
20 ml	**golden syrup**	1 tablespoon
25 g	**caster sugar**	1 OZ
25 g	**Bournville cocoa**	1 OZ
25 g	**'Rice Krispies'**	1 OZ
18-cm	**square shallow cake tin**	7-inch

A spoonful of seedless raisins or sultanas can be added to the 'krispie' mixture which can then be heaped into paper cake cases and left to set.

Too much cocoa. Not bad.

Sieve the flour into a bowl, add the sugar and rub in the butter. When the mixture will stick together, knead slightly then press evenly into the tin. Bake in a moderate oven (180°C, 350°F, Gas Mark 4) for 10–15 minutes. Turn out on to a wire tray.

Measure the butter, syrup, sugar and cocoa into a pan. Heat gently until melted completely. Stir in the 'Rice Krispies' and stir carefully until they are completely covered. Spread over the shortbread base and cut into oblongs.

Makes 10

Topsy-Turvy Bars

Illustrated on page 59

Metric		Imperial
150 g	**Bournville plain chocolate**	6 OZ
100 g	**soft margarine**	4 OZ
150 g	**caster sugar**	6 OZ
2	**eggs**	2
100 g	**sultanas**	4 OZ
200 g	**desiccated coconut**	8 OZ
100 g	**glacé cherries, chopped**	4 OZ
23-cm × 33-cm	**Swiss roll tin**	9-inch × 13-inch
	greaseproof paper	

Crumbly.

Grease the tin. Line the base with greaseproof paper and grease this too. Melt the chocolate carefully in a bowl over hot water then spread it evenly on the paper in the tin. Leave the chocolate in a cool place to harden again.

Cream the margarine and sugar together until they are lighter in colour and texture. Beat in the eggs then mix in the sultanas, coconut and chopped cherries. Spread the mixture evenly over the chocolate in the tin and bake in a moderate oven (180°C, 350°F, Gas Mark 4) for 20–30 minutes until golden brown on top. Leave in the tin until it is completely cool then turn out and peel off the paper. The chocolate should be hard. Cut down the centre then into 12 across. Serve the bars with the chocolate upwards.

Makes 24

Peppermint Squares

Illustrated on page 59

Metric		Imperial
175 g	**butter or hard margarine**	6 oz
175 g	**soft brown sugar**	6 oz
2	**eggs**	2
150 g	**self-raising flour**	5 oz
25 g	**Bournville cocoa**	1 oz
40 ml	**peppermint cordial**	2 tablespoons
40 ml	**water**	2 tablespoons
100 g	**caster sugar**	4 oz

23-cm × 33-cm	**Swiss roll tin, greased**	9-inch × 13-inch

Freeze the squares for up to 3 months. Put waxed paper between the squares and pack carefully. Wrap, seal and label. Defrost at room temperature.

Do not use *soft* margarine in this recipe as the consistency becomes too soft with it.

Soften the butter or margarine slightly to make it easier to beat in the soft brown sugar. Beat well until lighter in colour and texture then beat in the eggs. Sieve the flour and cocoa and stir into the mixture. Turn into the prepared tin and level the surface with a knife. Bake in a moderate oven (180°C, 350°F, Gas Mark 4) for 30–40 minutes. When cooked, the surface should be soft though set.

Mix the peppermint cordial with the water and the sugar. When the cake mixture is cooked, take it out of the oven and immediately spread the paste over the whole of the top surface. This makes a crisp crust when cold. Cut into squares.

Makes 24

Frosted Malted Bars

Illustrated on page 59

Metric		Imperial
100 g	margarine	4 oz
150 g	plain flour	6 oz
100 g	soft brown sugar	4 oz
	Filling	
25 g	plain flour	1 oz
2.5 ml	baking powder	½ teaspoon
25 g	Bournvita	1 oz
50 g	caster sugar	2 oz
2	eggs	2
5 ml	vanilla essence	1 teaspoon
50 g	desiccated coconut	2 oz
50 g	walnuts, chopped	2 oz
	Frosting	
50 g	Bournvita	2 oz
2.5 ml	instant coffee	½ teaspoon
40 ml	hot water	2 tablespoons
25 g	margarine or butter	1 oz
200 g	icing sugar, sieved	8 oz
2.5 ml	vanilla essence	½ teaspoon

Freeze complete.

A 19-cm/7½-inch square cake tin may also be used.

18-cm × 28-cm **shallow cake tin, greased** 7-inch × 11-inch

Rub the margarine into the flour then stir in the brown sugar. Press the mixture into the tin, prick the surface and bake in a moderate oven (180°C, 350°F, Gas Mark 4) for 10 minutes.

Meanwhile make the filling. Sieve the flour and baking powder into a bowl. Mix in the Bournvita, sugar, eggs, vanilla essence, coconut and walnuts. Spread this mixture evenly over the pastry in the tin and return to the oven for a further 25–30 minutes. Cool in the tin.

For the frosting, mix the Bournvita and coffee with the hot water. Beat in the margarine, sieved icing sugar and essence until really smooth. Spread frosting over the mixture in the tin and mark the surface with a fork. When set, cut into half down the centre and then across several times.

Makes 12 or 14

*Cherry Clusters (see page 64);
Ginger Shorties (see page 57);
Melting Moments (see
page 65); Chocolate Biscuits
(see page 64); Cottage Cookies
(see page 65)*

Chocolate Biscuits

Illustrated on page 63

Metric		Imperial
100 g	**butter or margarine**	4 oz
50 g	**caster sugar**	2 oz
	few drops of vanilla essence	
100 g	**plain flour, sieved**	4 oz
25 g	**Bournville cocoa, sieved**	1 oz
	pinch of salt	
	Butter icing	
75 g	**butter**	3 oz
150 g	**icing sugar, sieved**	6 oz
40 ml	**hot water**	2 tablespoons
	few drops vanilla essence (optional)	
	Decoration	
	little icing sugar	

baking tray, greased

Freeze the biscuits complete, or without the butter icing. Pack, label and seal. They crumble easily when thawed.

Dip the fork in water to prevent it sticking to the biscuit mixture.

Cream the butter and sugar together thoroughly. Add the essence and fold in the sieved flour and cocoa with a pinch of salt; it should all mix together quite well. Divide the mixture equally in half then each piece into six. Roll into balls and place them on a greased baking tray, spaced fairly well apart. Flatten each one with a fork, yet leave the mixture quite thick still. Bake in a moderately hot oven (190°C, 375°F, Gas Mark 5) for 12–15 minutes. Lift the biscuits on to a wire tray to cool when they have hardened slightly.

Beat the butter to soften it then beat in the sieved icing sugar and the water. It should be a nice light texture and colour. Vanilla essence can also be added. Sandwich the biscuits together with icing and dust with icing sugar.

Makes 6 complete biscuits

Cherry Clusters

Illustrated on page 63

Metric		Imperial
1 quantity	**Chocolate Biscuits mixture**	1 quantity
50 g	**glacé cherries, chopped**	2 oz

Mixed dried fruit or chopped nuts may also be added.

Add chopped cherries to the chocolate biscuit mixture. Spoon small heaps on to a greased baking tray and bake as for

Chocolate Biscuits. They may take a couple of minutes longer as the mixture is thicker.

Makes about 25

Melting Moments

Illustrated on page 63

Metric		Imperial
1 quantity	**Chocolate Biscuits mixture**	1 quantity
50 g	**porridge oats**	2 oz
6	**glacé cherries, halved**	6

Make up the chocolate biscuit mixture and roll into 12 balls. Roll these in the porridge oats. Place them on a greased baking tray and flatten a little with your fingers. Put half a glacé cherry in the centre of each biscuit. Bake as for Chocolate Biscuits.

Makes 12

Cottage Cookies

Illustrated on page 63

Freeze the cookies without the marmalade on top. Pack, label and seal.

The cookies can also be rolled in crushed cornflakes, or 'Rice Krispies'.

Metric		Imperial
100 g	**margarine**	4 oz
100 g	**caster sugar**	4 oz
2	**eggs**	2
175 g	**self-raising flour, sieved**	7 oz
25 g	**Cadbury's drinking chocolate**	1 oz
60 ml	**thick marmalade**	2 tablespoons
75 g	**porridge oats**	3 oz
	little extra marmalade peel	

baking tray, greased

Cream the margarine and sugar well together. Beat in the eggs. Fold in the sieved flour and drinking chocolate then the marmalade. Roll small spoonsful of the mixture in the porridge oats and place them on a greased baking tray, allowing room for them to spread. It may be necessary to do two traysful, or bake them in batches. Bake in a fairly hot oven (200°C, 400°F, Gas Mark 6) for about 15 minutes. They should be golden brown but will still be soft. Lift carefully on to a wire tray to cool. Decorate some of the cookies with pieces of marmalade peel.

Makes about 30

Viennese Fingers

Metric		Imperial
150 g	**butter**	6 oz
50 g	**caster sugar**	2 oz
100 g	**plain flour, sieved**	4 oz
25 g	**cornflour, sieved**	1 oz
25 g	**Bournville cocoa, sieved**	1 oz
	few drops of vanilla essence	
	Butter icing	
150 g	**icing sugar**	6 oz
25 g	**Bournville cocoa**	1 oz
75 g	**butter or soft margarine**	3 oz
20 ml	**warm water**	1 tablespoon
	Decoration	
	icing sugar, sieved	

piping bag and star vegetable pipe
baking tray, greased

Make up the biscuit mixture by softening the butter then creaming it with the sugar. Fold in the sieved flour, cornflour and cocoa then add a little vanilla essence. Mix all the ingredients together until the mixture is really well blended and fairly soft. Fill the piping bag then pipe lengths about 9 cm/$3\frac{1}{2}$ inches long on to a greased baking tray. There should be between 20 and 24. Make an even number if possible. Bake in a moderate oven (180°C, 350°F, Gas Mark 4) for 15 minutes. As the biscuits are quite short, leave them on the tray to harden before cooling completely.

Sieve the icing sugar and cocoa into a bowl. Beat in the butter and warm water, making a nice light consistency. Sandwich two of the finger biscuits together with a thick layer of the butter icing, which can be either spread or piped in between. Dredge with sieved icing sugar.

Makes about 12 complete biscuits

Chocolate Gems: Pipe the biscuits into small stars. Place a piece of glacé cherry in the centre and bake for 10 minutes. They can also be decorated with coloured glacé icing (see page 14).

Pack the fingers very carefully and freeze with or without the butter icing. Seal and label.

The finely grated rind of a small orange, or a lemon, may be added to the mixture. Use only the zest, never the white part which is bitter.

Florentines (see page 68);
Doboz Torte (see page 69)

TRADITIONAL FARE

Black Forest Gâteau and Florentines must surely be two of the most famous recipes in the world. You may have tasted them on holiday abroad or perhaps when eating out. These rich, delicious specialities are rather more expensive to prepare than some of the other recipes in the book but we have simplified them enough for you to try without fear of failure. Treat yourself, your family and your guests to the luxury of a rich chocolate cake or tempting dessert presented in the grand traditional manner.

Florentines

Illustrated on page 67

Metric		Imperial
50 g	**butter**	2 oz
50 g	**caster sugar**	2 oz
50 g	**blanched almonds**	2 oz
25 g	**glacé cherries**	1 oz
20 g	**flaked almonds**	$\frac{1}{2}$ oz
25 g	**mixed peel**	1 oz
40 ml	**whipped cream**	1 tablespoon
150 g	**Bournville plain chocolate**	6 oz
2	**baking trays**	2
	Bakewell paper	

Let the Florentines get completely cold before spreading with melted chocolate. It may be easier to put just a little on first to avoid the chocolate dripping through.

Melt the butter in a pan, stir in the sugar and bring slowly to the boil. Chop the blanched almonds small and the cherries into quarters. Mix the nuts in with the fruit and finally stir in the cream.

Cover the baking trays with Bakewell paper. Put teaspoonsful of the mixture on to the trays, spaced well apart, then flatten them down. Bake in a moderate oven (180°C, 350°F, Gas Mark 4) for 8–10 minutes until they are golden brown. Neaten the edges with a plain pastry cutter or knife. Cool slightly before lifting off the tray with a fish slice. Cook the remaining mixture in the same way.

Melt the chocolate and spread over the smooth side of each Florentine, covering them completely. Stand chocolate side up. When the chocolate begins to set, mark it with a fork to make swirls on the Florentines.

Makes 15

Doboz Torte

Illustrated on page 67

Metric		Imperial
3	**eggs**	3
100 g	**caster sugar**	4 oz
100 g	**plain flour**	4 oz
	pinch of salt	
150 g	**granulated sugar**	6 oz
	Butter icing	
200 g	**Bournville plain chocolate**	8 oz
200 g	**butter**	8 oz
400 g	**icing sugar, sieved**	1 lb

Caramel will not freeze. The cake layers can be assembled with the butter icing. Leave the top one plain and put the caramel on later. Wrap, label and seal. Freeze a little butter icing separately to finish off the cake.

The secret of making caramel successfully is to dissolve the sugar properly. Patience is necessary; wait until the liquid is quite clear.

piping bag and small star vegetable pipe

Make the cake layers the day before they are required. Have ready 5 flat surfaces, such as baking trays or roasting tins that are large enough for 18-cm/7-inch circles. Brush these with oil then dust with flour, shaking off any surplus. Mark a circle on each, using a cake tin or plate as a guide.

Whisk the eggs and caster sugar together in a bowl over hot water, or use an electric mixer. It will take at least 10 minutes to get the mixture thick enough to leave a definite trail. Sieve the flour with a pinch of salt into the mixture and fold in carefully so that the air is not knocked out. Divide the cake mixture evenly between the circles, spread them flat then bake in batches as necessary, in a moderately hot oven (190°C, 375°F, Gas Mark 5) for 6–8 minutes, until cooked through and pale golden brown. Lift off and cool on wire trays. Trim edges so that all the circles are the same size.

Place the granulated sugar in a heavy-based saucepan and just cover it with water. Dissolve the sugar over a very low heat, without stirring, so that the liquid becomes quite clear. Now bring to the boil and cook rapidly until the caramel turns a rich golden brown. Meanwhile lift one cake layer on to a lightly oiled baking tray. Pour the caramel over the cake, completely covering the top. When it is almost hard, mark with a knife into 12 sections. Trim edges if necessary.

Melt the chocolate in a bowl over a pan of hot water. Beat the butter then beat in the sieved icing sugar really well. Mix in the melted chocolate. Sandwich the cake layers together with some of the chocolate butter icing, putting the caramel layer on top. Lift the cake on to a plate or cake board. Attach a small star vegetable pipe to a piping bag and fill it with the remaining butter icing. Pipe zigzags down the side, all round the cake and stars round the top. The cake keeps well in a tin.

Devil's Food Cake

Illustrated opposite

Metric		Imperial
150 g	**plain flour**	6 oz
5 ml	**baking powder**	1 teaspoon
2.5 ml	**bicarbonate of soda**	½ teaspoon
50 g	**Bournville cocoa**	2 oz
100 g	**butter**	4 oz
200 g	**dark soft brown sugar**	8 oz
2	**eggs**	2
80 ml	**soured cream or plain yogurt**	4 tablespoons
	Frosting	
1	**egg white**	1
45 ml	**cold water**	3 tablespoons
175 g	**granulated sugar**	7 oz
1.25 ml	**cream of tartar**	¼ teaspoon
2.5 ml	**vanilla essence**	½ teaspoon
2 20-cm	**round shallow cake tins,**	2 8-inch
	greased and base lined	

Freeze the cake complete with the icing. Open freeze then pack later in a rigid container, seal and label.

The frosting has to be made over hot water so that the sugar can melt and give a smooth finish. If you find the cream of tartar difficult to measure, use a couple of good pinches.

Sieve the flour, baking powder and bicarbonate of soda. Mix the cocoa with just enough boiling water to make a smooth paste. Cream the butter and sugar together. Beat in the eggs then the soured cream or yogurt, cocoa and lastly, fold in the sieved dry ingredients. Divide the mixture evenly between the tins, level off the surface and bake in a moderately hot oven (190°C, 375°F, Gas Mark 5) for about 35 minutes. Turn out the cakes and cool on a wire tray, removing the paper lining first.

Place the egg white, water, sugar and cream of tartar into a fairly large bowl and stand this over a pan of hot water. Whisk hard with an electric hand mixer or a rotary whisk for at least 10 minutes, so that the mixture is glossy white, smooth and will stand in peaks. The whisking becomes very stiff to do but the frosting will not harden at all if it does not reach the correct consistency. Add the vanilla essence when the frosting is ready.

Sandwich the cakes together with frosting, lift on to a plate and cover with the remaining frosting, being careful not to get any chocolate cake crumbs into it. Leave the cake for an hour or so as the frosting forms a crust while the inside remains soft. This cake keeps exceptionally well in an airtight tin.

Devil's Food Cake (see above); Brownies (see page 73)

Black Forest Gâteau

Metric		Imperial
	Shortbread base	
50 g	butter	2 oz
25 g	caster sugar	1 oz
75 g	plain flour	3 oz
	Cake mixture	
100 g	soft margarine or butter	4 oz
100 g	caster sugar	4 oz
2	eggs	2
75 g	self-raising flour, sieved	3 oz
25 g	Bournville cocoa, sieved	1 oz
	Filling and decoration	
2 425-g cans	black cherries	2 15-oz cans
30 ml	kirsch or cherry brandy	2 tablespoons
40 ml	red jam	2 tablespoons
250 ml	double cream	$\frac{1}{2}$ pint
125 ml	single cream	$\frac{1}{4}$ pint
75 g	Bournville plain chocolate	3 oz
12	chocolate shapes (see page 10)	12
23-cm	cake tin, greased	9-inch
	greaseproof paper piping bag	
	piping bag and star pipe	

Use fresh cherries when they are in season. Cans of black cherries are sometimes difficult to buy so substitute red cherries, or try a mixture of both.

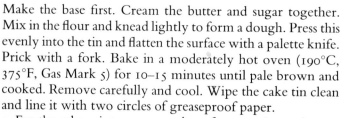

Make the base first. Cream the butter and sugar together. Mix in the flour and knead lightly to form a dough. Press this evenly into the tin and flatten the surface with a palette knife. Prick with a fork. Bake in a moderately hot oven (190°C, 375°F, Gas Mark 5) for 10–15 minutes until pale brown and cooked. Remove carefully and cool. Wipe the cake tin clean and line it with two circles of greaseproof paper.

For the cake mixture, cream the soft margarine and sugar together. Beat in the eggs one at a time then fold in the sieved flour and cocoa. Spread the mixture evenly in the tin and bake in the moderately hot oven, at the same temperature, for 20–25 minutes until cooked. Turn out and cool on a wire tray.

Drain the juice from the cherries and add the kirsch to the liquid. Remove the cherry stones. Slice the cake through the centre, place the layers on plates and moisten with the cherry juice. Spread the jam on the pastry base. Whip the creams together until the cream holds its shape. Spread one cake layer with cream. Reserve 12 cherries and spread the remainder over the cream. Press the other cake layer on top and lift the whole cake on to the pastry base. Cover the cake with cream, keeping a little for the decoration, spreading it as flat as possible. Grate the chocolate then coat the sides of the cake with it. Melt any remaining in a small bowl over a pan of hot, not boiling water. Fill the paper piping bag. Cut the tip off the end. Mark the cake into 12 sections and pipe a zigzag pattern of chocolate on alternate sections. Place the remaining cream into the piping bag and pipe whirls on each section and one in the centre. Complete the cake by arranging the cherry halves and the chocolate shapes on alternate sections. Carefully lift the cake on to a plate or cake board.

Serves 12

Brownies

Illustrated on page 71

Metric		Imperial
150 g	**margarine**	6 oz
60 ml	**Bournville cocoa**	2 tablespoons
150 g	**caster or soft brown sugar**	6 oz
2	**eggs**	2
50 g	**self-raising flour, sieved**	2 oz
50 g	**walnuts, chopped**	2 oz
18-cm	**square cake tin,**	7-inch
	greased and base lined	

Melt 50 g/2 oz of the margarine in a pan, stir in the cocoa and set aside. Cream the remaining margarine with the sugar until lighter in colour then gradually beat in the eggs. Fold in the sieved flour then the chopped walnuts and the cocoa mixture. Turn into the prepared tin, smooth the surface and bake in a moderate oven (180°C, 350°F, Gas Mark 4) for about 45 minutes until cooked. Cool in the tin. Later, turn out and cut into squares.

Makes 12 or 16

Soufflé

Illustrated on page 79

Metric		Imperial
400 ml	milk	¾ pint
30 g	Bournville cocoa	1½ oz
75 g	caster sugar	3 oz
3 size 2	eggs, separated	3 large
275 ml	double cream	½ pint
14 g	gelatine	½ oz
80 ml	water	4 tablespoons
50 g	Bournville plain chocolate	2 oz
	greaseproof paper	
550-ml	soufflé dish	1-pint
	piping bag and star pipe	

Prepare the dish first. Tie a double band of greaseproof paper round the dish, allowing sufficient height for it to come at least 5 cm/2 inches above the rim. Use a double piece of string, put the ends through the loop, separate the pieces and tie up at the other side (see photograph 1, opposite). Grease the dish and paper very lightly.

Bring the milk and the cocoa to the boil, stirring to dissolve the cocoa. Cream the sugar and egg yolks together then stir in the chocolate milk. Return to the pan and heat gently, stirring continuously until the custard thickens. Do not allow the egg custard to boil. Cool a little in the pan.

Whip half the cream and stir into the custard. Dissolve the gelatine in the water and when it is quite clear, pour it into the custard, making sure they are both at the same temperature. Cool the custard fairly quickly by placing the bowl or pan on ice, or in the freezer if you watch it. Avoid getting the custard too thick. When it is just beginning to set, whisk the egg whites until they are at the soft peak stage and fold into the custard (see photograph 2, opposite). Quickly pour the mixture into the prepared soufflé dish and leave to set.

Remove the paper band by pressing a palette knife against the side of the dish and peeling back the paper (see photograph 3, opposite). Whip the remaining cream. Spread cream round the soufflé edge and spoon the remainder into the piping bag. Grate the chocolate, spread it on a large piece of greaseproof paper and stand the dish in the centre. Flick the chocolate up on to the sides, covering them completely (see photograph 4, opposite). Complete the soufflé by piping whirls round the top.

Serves 6

Do not decorate. Open freeze the soufflé in the paper collar. When firm, wrap in foil then polythene; label and seal. Allow about 4 hours for it to thaw then decorate.

When adding egg whites to soufflés, do not whisk them too hard or they will be difficult to fold in. It is sometimes easier to stir a good spoonful of the chocolate mixture into the egg whites, then fold the egg whites into the chocolate.

The soufflé dish can be lined with Bakewell paper, in which case there will be no need to grease it.

Ideally, a soufflé is better eaten the same day but it can be kept overnight.

1 Tie a double band of greaseproof paper round the dish to make a collar. Secure with string. If desired, lightly grease the dish and paper collar.

2 Fold the beaten egg whites into the chocolate custard, using a metal spoon or spatula.

3 Press a long, flat-bladed knife straight against the side of the dish and carefully peel off the paper, keeping the knife against the soufflé.

4 Spread soufflé edge with whipped cream. Stand the dish in a circle of grated Bournville plain chocolate and flick up on to the cream. Decorate with whipped cream.

Orange and Chocolate Soufflé

When making the Soufflé mixture on page 74, add the finely grated rind and the juice of 1 orange to the eggs and sugar.

Hot Chocolate Soufflé

Metric		Imperial
50 g	**butter**	2 oz
50 g	**plain flour**	2 oz
20 ml	**Bournville cocoa**	1 tablespoon
275 ml	**milk**	$\frac{1}{2}$ pint
3	**eggs, separated**	3
50 g	**caster sugar**	2 oz
	Decoration	
	little icing sugar	
	greaseproof paper	
1.2-litre	**soufflé dish, buttered**	2-pint

Depending on the shape of the soufflé dish, it may not always be necessary to tie a paper collar round it. A deeper dish forces the mixture upwards and it will come higher above the rim of the dish, so needs the support of a paper collar.

If the roux is lumpy after the milk has been added, whisk quickly with a rotary whisk and the lumps will disappear.

Line the dish with a paper collar as described in the Soufflé recipe, page 74.

Melt the butter in a saucepan and stir in the flour and cocoa, making a roux. Beat and cook the mixture until it comes away from the sides of the pan. Stir in the milk and continue cooking until the milk is absorbed and is thickened into a sauce. Cool slightly before adding the egg yolks, one at a time, off the heat. Whisk the egg whites to the soft peak stage then whisk in the sugar until it is as stiff again. Fold carefully into the chocolate sauce and turn the mixture into the soufflé dish. Stand the dish in a roasting tin half filled with water. Cook in a fairly hot oven (200°C, 400°F, Gas Mark 6) for about 50 minutes. The soufflé should be well risen with a slight crust on the top. Dust with icing sugar and serve immediately. Single cream is nice with the soufflé but it is not essential.

Serves 4

Roulade

The roll will probably crack on the top when it is rolled up but this is hidden by the extra icing sugar. The texture is heavier than a Swiss roll so you will need a fork to eat it with.

Metric		Imperial
100 g	**Bournville plain chocolate**	4 oz
3	**eggs, separated**	3
100 g	**caster sugar**	4 oz
30 ml	**hot water**	2 tablespoons
275 ml	**whipping cream**	$\frac{1}{2}$ pint
	icing sugar, sieved	

35-cm × 25-cm	**Swiss roll tin, greased**	14-inch × 10-inch
	greaseproof paper	

Line the Swiss roll tin with greaseproof paper and brush the paper lining well with oil. Melt the chocolate in a bowl over hot water. Whisk the egg yolks and caster sugar together until they are light in colour and texture. Stir the hot water into the melted chocolate then mix this with the egg yolks. Whisk the egg whites stiffly and fold them carefully into the mixture. Pour the mixture into the prepared tin and spread it lightly and evenly into all the corners, so that the surface is as flat as possible, without knocking out the air in the egg whites. Place in the centre of a moderate oven (180°C, 350°F, Gas Mark 4) for 15–20 minutes. Prick a warm skewer into the centre which should come out clean. Leave the mixture in the tin. Cover it with a piece of greaseproof paper and a damp tea towel on top. Leave undisturbed for at least 3 hours, or overnight, keeping the tea towel damp so it will not crisp up.

Whip the cream until it will just hold its shape. Dust a large piece of greaseproof paper with sieved icing sugar and turn out the mixture from the tin on to it. Peel off the paper lining. Spread the cream over the surface and roll up from the short side, like a Swiss roll, using the large piece of greaseproof paper to help. Dust with extra icing sugar. Lift on to a plate and chill the roulade for an hour before eating.

Serves about 6

Chocolate Pots

Illustrated opposite

Metric		Imperial
550 ml	**milk**	1 pint
100 g	**Bournville plain chocolate**	4 oz
2	**eggs**	2
2	**egg yolks**	2
25 g	**caster sugar**	1 oz
10 ml	**rum or cointreau**	2 teaspoons
80 ml	**whipped cream**	4 tablespoons

Heat the milk in a saucepan, melting all but one of the squares of chocolate in it at the same time. Beat the eggs, egg yolks and sugar in a bowl. When the chocolate is completely melted, pour the hot but not boiling milk on to the eggs, stirring all the time. Add the rum. Strain the chocolate custard back into the clean pan, or into a jug, and divide the custard between 4 or 5 individual ovenproof dishes.

Half fill a roasting tin with warm water. Put the dishes into this, being careful to see that the water cannot come over the top, and bake them in a warm oven (160°C, 325°F, Gas Mark 3) for 40–60 minutes. The custard should be lightly set. Serve the custards hot or cold. Decorate with a spoonful of cream on top and grated chocolate, using the remaining square.

Serves 4 or 5

Chocolate Mousse

Illustrated on page 83

Metric		Imperial
75 g	**Bournville plain chocolate**	3 oz
3	**eggs, separated**	3
	Decoration	
	grated Bournville chocolate	

Break the chocolate into a medium-sized bowl and melt it over a pan of hot water. Stir in the egg yolks, off the heat. Whisk the egg whites stiffly and fold into the chocolate, making sure that it is all folded in. Turn the mousse into a glass dish or divide it between individual sundae glasses. Leave in the refrigerator for a couple of hours at least. Sprinkle with a little grated chocolate before serving.

Serves 3–4

To extend the mousse, whip 125 ml/¼ pint double cream and fold into the chocolate and egg yolks, before adding the egg whites. A little rum or brandy may also be added.

The mousse is excellent eaten the day after it is made.

Soufflé (see page 74); Chocolate Pots (see above)

Choux Pastry

Metric		Imperial
125 ml	**water**	$\frac{1}{4}$ pint
50 g	**butter or margarine**	2 oz
2	**eggs**	2
65 g	**plain flour, sieved**	$2\frac{1}{2}$ oz

Measure the water and butter into a saucepan. Melt the butter gently then increase the heat and bring to the boil. Immediately take the pan off the heat and shoot in the flour all at once. Stir the mixture. Beat the eggs together and add a little at a time to the pan, beating hard with a wooden spoon between each addition. If the eggs are very large, the mixture may become too soft so do not add it all. The pastry should come cleanly away from the sides of the pan and have a really glossy appearance. The mixture can be left at this stage.

Éclairs

Metric		Imperial
1 quantity	**choux pastry (see above)**	1 quantity
125 ml	**double cream**	$\frac{1}{4}$ pint
50 g	**Bournville plain chocolate**	2 oz
13 g	**butter**	$\frac{1}{2}$ oz
20 ml	**water**	1 tablespoon
25 g	**icing sugar**	1 oz
	piping bag and plain 1.5-cm/$\frac{3}{4}$-inch pipe	
2	**baking trays, greased and lightly floured**	2

Make up the choux pastry as described. Fill the piping bag. Pipe the choux pastry into lengths, making 10 to 12, depending on the size. Space them well apart, allowing room for them to rise. Bake in a moderate oven (180°C, 350°F, Gas Mark 4) for 10 minutes then increase the heat to moderately hot (190°C, 375°F, Gas Mark 5) for another 10 minutes. Finally, increase the heat to fairly hot (200°C, 400°F, Gas Mark 6) for another 10 minutes, by which time the éclairs should be well risen, golden brown and firm. Cool on a wire tray, making a small slit in the side of each éclair to let the steam escape.

Whip the cream and fill the éclairs with it. Melt the chocolate and butter with the water in a pan over a gentle

Uncooked choux pastry may be kept for 24 hours in the refrigerator, ready to be cooked when required. As an alternative, fill the éclairs with the Cream Puffs filling (see page 42). Omit the chocolate icing but sprinkle with icing sugar.

heat, stirring continuously. Sieve the icing sugar into a bowl and beat the melted chocolate into it, stirring until smooth. Spread the cold icing on each éclair. Ideally, they should be eaten the same day as choux pastry goes soft after being filled.

Makes 10–12

Profiteroles

To make round buns, rub over the top of each with a wetted finger to smooth the surface.

Metric		Imperial
1 quantity	**choux pastry (see page 80)**	1 quantity
125 ml	**double cream**	¼ pint
20 ml	**caster or icing sugar**	1 tablespoon
	few drops of vanilla essence	
	Sauce	
50 g	**Bournville plain chocolate**	2 oz
45 ml	**water**	3 tablespoons
10 ml	**cornflour**	2 teaspoons
10 ml	**sugar**	2 teaspoons
125 ml	**milk**	¼ pint
80 ml	**single cream**	4 tablespoons
	few drops of vanilla essence	

piping bag and 1.5-cm/¾-inch plain vegetable pipe
baking tray, greased and floured

Make up the choux pastry and fill the piping bag. Pipe small mounds of the mixture on to the prepared tray, making about 25 in all. Bake in a moderate oven (180°C, 350°F, Gas Mark 4) for 10 minutes. Increase the heat to moderately hot (190°C, 375°F, Gas Mark 5) for another 10 minutes and finally increase the heat to fairly hot (200°C, 400°F, Gas Mark 6) for about 5 minutes until the choux buns are golden brown and crisp. Make a small slit in the side to let out the steam and cool on a wire tray.

Whip the cream with the sugar and vanilla essence until it will just hold its shape. Fill the piping bag and squeeze cream into each of the buns. Pile them into a dish.

Make the sauce by melting the chocolate in the water, over a gentle heat, in a saucepan. Blend the cornflour and sugar with a little milk, then add the rest of it and empty into the saucepan. Add the chocolate. Stir until the custard comes to the boil and thickens. Cool the sauce a little before adding the cream and vanilla essence. Either have the chocolate sauce hot or cold, poured over the profiteroles.

Serves about 8

Fondue

Illustrated on page 119

Metric		Imperial
200 g	**Bournville plain chocolate**	8 oz
80 ml	**fresh orange juice**	4 tablespoons
I	**small can evaporated milk, chilled**	I
	grated rind of ½ orange	
	fresh fruit	

Melt the chocolate, broken into squares, with the orange juice and 60 ml/3 tablespoons of the evaporated milk in a fondue dish, or in a bowl over a pan of hot water. Stir occasionally until smooth. Whisk the remaining evaporated milk until it is quite thick then fold into the chocolate mixture. Return to the heat and keep warm. Serve with a selection of prepared fresh fruit and, perhaps, some sponge finger biscuits.

For an even richer fondue, melt the Bournville plain chocolate with 120 ml/ 6 tablespoons double cream and 40 ml/2 tablespoons of rum.

Use fondue forks or cocktail sticks to dip the fruit in the fondue.

St. Emilion au Chocolat

Illustrated opposite

Metric		Imperial
200 g	**Bournville plain chocolate**	8 oz
100 g	**ratafia biscuits**	4 oz
40 ml	**rum**	2 tablespoons
100 g	**slightly salted butter**	4 oz
100 g	**caster sugar**	4 oz
250 ml	**milk**	½ pint
2	**eggs**	2
40 ml	**whipped cream**	2 tablespoons

Serve a dish of poached fruit or fresh fruit salad with this rich chocolate pudding.

Melt the chocolate in a bowl over a pan of hot water. Soak the ratafias in the rum. Cream the butter and sugar together then add the melted chocolate. Put the milk and the eggs into a saucepan and stir over a gentle heat to thicken the custard enough to coat the back of a wooden spoon. Be careful not to boil it. Slowly pour the custard into the chocolate mixture, stirring continuously. Leave in a cold place, preferably a refrigerator, until it is beginning to thicken and set. Spoon half the mixture into a glass dish and cover with a layer of ratafias, leaving out some for the top. Cover the biscuits with the remaining chocolate mixture. Swirl the cream through the centre and arrange the remaining ratafias round the edge. Refrigerate the pudding for several hours until required.

Serves 6–8

St. Emilion au Chocolat (see above); Chocolate Mousse (see page 78); Bavarian Cream (see page 97)

Sacher Torte

Metric		Imperial
150 g	**Bournville plain chocolate**	6 oz
125 g	**butter**	5 oz
125 g	**caster sugar**	5 oz
6 size 2	**eggs, separated**	6 large
125 g	**plain flour, sieved**	5 oz
	Icing	
75 g	**Bournville plain chocolate**	3 oz
25 g	**butter**	1 oz
60 ml	**water**	4 tablespoons
325 g	**icing sugar**	12 oz
	gravy browning or brown food colouring	
20-cm	**round deep cake tin, greased and base lined**	8-inch

Freeze the cake complete. Pack, label and freeze.

This is an unusual recipe with no raising agent. It is therefore particularly important to whisk the egg whites stiffly and fold them into the mixture, being careful to avoid knocking out the air.

Melt the chocolate for the cake mixture in a bowl standing over a pan of hot water. Cream the butter with only 75 g/3 oz of the sugar. Beat in the egg yolks and the melted chocolate. Fold in the sieved flour. Whisk all the egg whites together in a large bowl so that they are really stiff. Add the remaining 50 g/2 oz of sugar and whisk again until they are as stiff. Stir a little into the chocolate mixture to loosen the texture then fold in the remaining egg whites. Turn into the tin and bake in a moderate oven (180°C, 350°F, Gas Mark 4) for 1 hour–1 hour 10 minutes. Test with a warm skewer to see if the cake is cooked through. Turn out and cool on a wire tray.

Make the icing by melting the chocolate with the butter and water in saucepan over gentle heat, stirring continuously. Sieve the icing sugar into a large bowl, make a well in the centre and gradually stir in the liquid chocolate. Beat the icing until smooth and cool so that it is thick enough to spread on the cake. Cover the top and sides of the cake, leaving it quite rough so that the icing swirls attractively. Blend a little gravy browning with the scraps of icing, put it in a paper piping bag and pipe the words 'Sacher Torte' over the top. Lift the cake on to a plate.

Whisked Sponge

Metric		Imperial
3	**eggs**	3
75 g	**caster sugar**	3 oz
75 g	**plain flour**	3 oz
30 ml	**Bournville cocoa**	2 tablespoons
	Filling	
	strawberry or apricot jam	
125 ml	**whipping cream**	$\frac{1}{4}$ pint
	Decoration	
	caster or icing sugar	
2 18-cm	**sandwich cake tins,**	2 7-inch
	greased and base lined	

The cakes are generally better frozen without the filling but can be completed, packed carefully and frozen for a limited period. Sponges keep well if packed with a piece of greaseproof paper between them.

Whisked sponge mixtures can be difficult to make as the result depends on the amount of air beaten into the mixture. If you repeatedly have difficulty, add 5 ml/1 level teaspoon baking powder, sieved with the flour and cocoa.

To make a quick decoration, lay a pretty paper doily on top of the sponge and dust with icing sugar. Carefully lift off the doily and the pattern will be left on the cake. These cakes should be quite deep and slightly larger tins may be used if less depth is preferred.

Place the eggs and sugar in a fairly large bowl, over a pan of hot, not boiling water. An electric mixer is ideal to use here. Whisk until the mixture is really stiff and will leave a good trail; it will take between 10 and 20 minutes by hand. Sieve the flour and cocoa together then sieve it again into the bowl. Fold in carefully so that there are no pockets of flour left. Divide the mixture between the tins and level off the surface by tilting the tins. Do not touch the tops with a knife or spatula as this could knock out some of the air that has been beaten in so carefully. Put the cakes into the centre of a fairly hot oven (200°C, 400°F, Gas Mark 6) for about 15 minutes until they are cooked and spring back when touched. Turn the cakes out on to a wire tray, remove the paper linings and immediately turn them over so that there are no marks on the top. Leave the cakes to cool.

Spread one cake liberally with jam. Whip the cream and spread this on top. Sandwich the two cakes together and dust with caster sugar or sieved icing sugar. Lift on to a plate.

Swiss Roll

Illustrated opposite

Metric		Imperial
3 size 2	**eggs**	3 large
75 g	**caster sugar**	3 oz
	few drops of vanilla essence	
75 g	**plain flour**	3 oz
25 g	**Bournville cocoa**	1 oz
15 ml	**warm water**	1 tablespoon
	Decoration	
125 ml	**double cream or**	¼ pint
175 g	**vanilla butter icing**	6 oz
	(see page 14)	
3	**small Cadbury's Flakes**	3
35-cm × 25-cm	**Swiss roll tin,**	14-inch × 10-inch
	greased and lined	
	greaseproof paper	

The Swiss roll may be frozen complete. Pack carefully, label and freeze. Cream is better used within 1 month.

The filling can be varied in several ways. For simplicity, spread with jam. As a dessert, fill with cream and fruit. Bananas and chocolate cream are particularly delicious.

Whisk the eggs, sugar and vanilla essence in a large bowl placed over a pan of hot, not boiling water. Whisk until the mixture is thick enough to leave a good trail. You should be able to write your initials in it (see photograph 1, opposite). An electric mixer may be used when there is no need to beat over hot water. Sieve the flour and cocoa together and carefully fold into the mixture (see photograph 2, opposite), with the warm water. Turn the mixture into the prepared tin and level off the surface by tilting the tin. Do not touch the surface. Bake in a fairly hot oven (200°C, 400°F, Gas Mark 6) for 10–12 minutes.

Dust a large piece of greaseproof paper with caster sugar. Turn the Swiss roll out on to this and carefully peel off the paper lining. Trim off the hard edges. Mark a dent along one short side about 1 cm/½ inch from the edge and carefully roll up the Swiss roll, with the paper inside (see photograph 3, opposite). Leave the cake in the paper, on a wire tray.

Unroll the Swiss roll carefully and spread with whipped cream or the butter icing. Lay the Flakes end to end along the dent and roll up quite tightly. Decorate with cream and pieces of Flake, cut with a sharp knife (see photograph 4, opposite).

1 Whisk until mixture is thick enough to leave a visible trail.

2 Fold in the flour and Bournville cocoa sieved together, using a light wrist action. Make sure no pockets of flour are left.

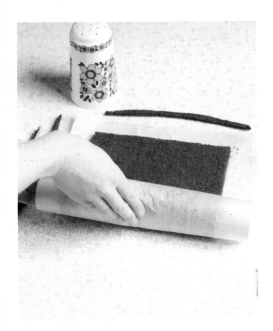

3 Turn the Swiss roll out on to a piece of sugared paper, trim the edges and roll up with the paper inside.

4 Fill and decorate the Swiss roll with whipped cream and Cadbury's Flakes.

PERFECT PUDDINGS

Most of us, I suspect, have a secret hankering for a 'super pud' at the end of a meal. Surely this is the course where appearances count most and can greatly influence our choice. However, it is most disappointing if the taste does not live up to the visual expectations. We often neglect the pudding course as being too much trouble; browse through this chapter and you will find there is no excuse. Here are puddings for the family, Sunday lunch or for that special occasion. Some are cooked in the oven, some prepared in a flash, or even left overnight to leave you free on a busy day. Let your imagination run riot and enjoy a superb chocolate dessert.

Castle Puddings

Illustrated on page 91

Metric		Imperial
100 g	**self-raising flour**	4 oz
2	**eggs**	2
100 g	**soft margarine**	4 oz
100 g	**light soft brown sugar**	4 oz
20 ml	**Bournville cocoa**	1 tablespoon
2.5 ml	**vanilla or orange essence**	½ teaspoon

about 15 dariole moulds, well greased

Sieve the flour into a bowl. Add the eggs, margarine and sugar. Beat the ingredients well together until they are completely blended. Divide the mixture in half. Mix the cocoa with a very little boiling water and add this to one amount. Stir the essence into the other. Drop alternate spoonsful of the mixtures into the moulds so that they are just over half full. Depending on the size, there will be between 12 and 15. Cover each one with a small piece of foil. Put them into a steamer placed over a pan of hot water and cook for about 30 minutes. The water should bubble gently and must not be allowed to run dry. Alternatively, the puddings may be cooked in the oven, in the same way as the Owl Madeleines (see page 46) when they can be cooked in batches. Serve with thin custard.

Makes about 15

The puddings can be frozen but will take some time to reheat, so it is only worth it if there is extra cake mixture to be used up perhaps.

Dariole moulds are sometimes called castle pudding tins. Larger individual tins may be used but the cooking time must be increased correspondingly.

Steamed Chocolate Pudding

Choose a taller basin if you have one so the pudding turns out an attractive shape.

Metric		Imperial
100 g	margarine	4 oz
100 g	caster sugar	4 oz
2	eggs	2
25 g	Bournville cocoa	1 oz
125 g	self-raising flour	5 oz
750-ml	pudding basin, greased	1½-pint
	greaseproof paper or foil	

Cream the margarine and sugar together. Add the eggs, one at a time. Dissolve the cocoa in a very little boiling water and add to the mixture. Fold in the flour. Turn into the pudding basin. Cover with a double layer of greaseproof paper or a piece of foil. Secure. Place in a steamer over a pan of hot water, or into a large saucepan half filled with hot water. Cover and steam for about 1½ hours; the timing is not too crucial as the pudding will wait until you are ready. It may also be cooked in a pressure cooker. Follow the manufacturers instructions but it will normally take about 50 minutes at Low (5-lb) pressure.

Turn out on to a warm plate and serve with custard, single cream or a sweet white sauce.

Serves 4–5

Orange Ring Pudding

Illustrated on page 91

Metric		Imperial
1 quantity	**Steamed Chocolate Pudding mixture**	1 quantity
2	oranges	2

Make up the chocolate pudding mixture. Add the finely grated rind of one orange. (The juice can be used instead of the water, if preferred.) Slice the other orange into circles and line the greased pudding basin with them, placing one on the bottom so that it will look nice when turned out. Cover and steam.

Serves 4–5

Layered Steamed Pudding

Make up the Steamed Chocolate Pudding mixture on page 89, only adding the Bournville cocoa to half the mixture. Leave the other half plain or add a few drops of orange, vanilla or peppermint essence. Place the mixture in alternate layers in the bowl. Cover and steam as described.

Topsy~Turvy Pudding

Metric		Imperial
425-g can	**pears or pineapple rings**	15-oz can
40 ml	**golden syrup**	2 tablespoons
about 8	**glacé cherries**	about 8
100 g	**margarine**	4 oz
100 g	**soft brown sugar**	4 oz
2	**eggs**	2
100 g	**self-raising flour, sieved**	4 oz
50 ml	**Cadbury's chocolate spread**	2 tablespoons
5–10 ml	**arrowroot**	1–2 teaspoons
20-cm	**round cake tin, greased**	8-inch

Drain the juice from the fruit and keep aside. Mix the golden syrup with a spoonful of the juice and pour into the cake tin. Arrange the pear halves or pineapple rings in the tin, with a cherry in the centre of each. Cream the margarine and sugar together. Gradually beat in the eggs and fold in the sieved flour. Mix the chocolate spread with a spoonful of the fruit juice and swirl this through the mixture. Carefully spread over the fruit in the tin and level off the surface. Bake in a moderately hot oven (190°C, 375°F, Gas Mark 5) for about 45 minutes. Turn out the pudding on to a hot plate and serve with the sauce.

Blend the arrowroot with a little of the remaining juice, in a saucepan. Add all the juice and bring the sauce to the boil while stirring continuously. Chocolate spread may be added if a chocolate sauce is preferred with the pudding.

Serves 5

The pudding may be frozen although it is at its best when eaten fresh.

Make the pudding in a smaller size tin if preferred, when the cooking time should be increased by 5–10 minutes. If made with white sugar the chocolate spread gives a marbled effect, but the flavour of the pudding is better with soft brown sugar.

Orange Ring Pudding (see page 89); Castle Puddings (see page 88); Chocolate Bakewell Tart (see page 92)

Chocolate Bakewell Tart

Illustrated on page 91

Metric		Imperial
	Pastry case	
50 g	margarine	2 oz
25 g	white fat	1 oz
125 g	plain flour	5 oz
	Filling	
75 g	jam	3 tablespoons
50 g	self-raising flour	2 oz
30 ml	Bournville cocoa	1 tablespoon
50 g	margarine	2 oz
50 g	caster sugar	2 oz
1	egg	1
25 g	ground almonds	1 oz
2.5 ml	almond essence	$\frac{1}{2}$ teaspoon
	finely grated rind of $\frac{1}{2}$ lemon	

18-cm	flan ring, on a baking tray	7-inch

Make up the pastry by rubbing the fats into the flour, until the mixture resembles breadcrumbs. Add just enough cold water to bind the mixture together. Knead lightly and roll out the pastry on a floured board. Line the flan ring, being careful not to stretch the pastry or it will shrink. Keep the scraps for the trellis. Spread the jam in the base.

Sieve the flour and cocoa. Cream the margarine and sugar together and slowly beat in the egg. Fold in the sieved flour and cocoa and stir in the ground almonds, essence and the grated lemon rind. Spread the mixture evenly in the pastry case. Roll out the scraps of pastry, cut strips and arrange them in a trellis across the top. Stick the ends on to the flan with a little water. Bake in a fairly hot oven (200°C, 400°F, Gas Mark 6) for 15 minutes then reduce the heat to moderate (180°C, 350°F, Gas Mark 4) for a further 15 minutes or until cooked. Serve hot or cold.

Serves 6

Wrap, label, seal and freeze the flan.

It is often handy to have pastry ready to use quickly. Measure out two or three times the basic recipe, rub the fats into the flour but do not add the water. Keep the rubbed-in mixture in a closed plastic container in the refrigerator, to use when required. It will keep for 2 months.

Veiled Apple Maidens

Illustrated on page 95

Fresh raspberries in season are particularly good in this recipe. Decorate with raspberries on top and mix some with the apples, or stew the raspberries lightly and use on their own.

Metric		Imperial
425-g can	**raspberries**	15-oz can
450 g	**cooking apples**	1 lb
25 g	**butter**	1 oz
30 ml	**sugar**	1 heaped tablespoon
150 g	**fresh brown breadcrumbs**	6 oz
75 g	**demerara sugar**	3 oz
20 ml	**Bournvita**	1 tablespoon
75 g	**Bournville plain chocolate**	3 oz
125 ml	**double cream**	$\frac{1}{4}$ pint
80 ml	**top of the milk**	4 tablespoons
	or single cream	
6	**individual sundae glasses or a**	6
20-cm	**flan ring**	8-inch

This recipe can be served in individual glasses or as one ring.

Drain the raspberries and put about 60 ml/3 tablespoons of the juice into a saucepan. Peel, core and slice the apples. Add the apple slices to the pan with the butter and sugar. Stew carefully then purée the apple and cool. Mix the breadcrumbs, demerara sugar and Bournvita together. Grate the chocolate coarsely and add two-thirds. Whip the cream and top of the milk together. Spoon some of the breadcrumb mixture into each of the glasses. Add the raspberries to the apple purée and divide this between the glasses. Spread a thin layer of cream in each. Finish off with another layer of breadcrumbs. Leave the puddings at this stage until they are required.

Decorate with a spoonful of cream on each glass and the remaining chocolate.

If making one dish only, place the greased flan dish on a suitable sized serving plate. Press half the breadcrumb mixture on to the base then add the fruit. Spread a thin layer of cream over the top. Repeat the breadcrumb layer. Finish off by masking the top with all the remaining cream. Leave the pudding in the flan ring until it is required. Decorate with the grated chocolate.

This pudding is better made well in advance so that the fruit can soak into the breadcrumb mixture.

Serves 6

Chocolate Queen of Puddings

Illustrated opposite

Metric		Imperial
550 ml	**milk**	1 pint
50 g	**butter**	2 oz
50 g	**Cadbury's drinking chocolate**	2 oz
100 g	**fresh breadcrumbs**	4 oz
3	**eggs, separated**	3
about 60 ml	**lemon curd**	2 rounded tablespoons
150 g	**caster sugar**	6 oz
750-ml	**pie dish, greased with butter**	1½-pint

Heat the milk with the butter and drinking chocolate. Place the breadcrumbs in the dish. Beat the egg yolks into the milk then pour over the breadcrumbs. Leave to stand for about 30 minutes if possible. Bake in a moderate oven (180°C, 350°F, Gas Mark 4) for about 40 minutes until set.

Spread the top with the lemon curd, or jam may be used. Whisk the egg whites really stiffly, fold in half the sugar and whisk again. Fold in the remaining sugar and pile the meringue on top of the base. Increase oven to very hot (230°C, 450°F, Gas Mark 8). Cook for about 5 minutes.

Serves 4

Bread Fingers

too much milk

Illustrated opposite

Metric		Imperial
250 ml	**milk**	½ pint
25 g	**Cadbury's drinking chocolate**	1 oz
1	**egg**	1
6	**thick, large slices of bread**	6
	oil for frying	
50 g	**caster sugar**	2 oz
	assorted jam	

Whisk the milk and drinking chocolate together in a saucepan while warming it. Off the heat, whisk in the egg. Cut the crusts off the bread slices then cut each slice into three finger shapes. Dip the bread fingers into the chocolate custard. Fry them on both sides in hot shallow oil, in a frying pan. Drain on kitchen paper. Dust with caster sugar and place a spoon of jam in the centre of each finger. Serve hot.

Makes 18

Mix a little ground cinnamon with the caster sugar.

Chocolate Queen of Puddings (see above); Veiled Apple Maidens (see page 93); Bread Fingers (see above)

Hungarian Chocolate Mousse

Metric		Imperial
75 g	**Bournville plain chocolate**	3 oz
15 ml	**instant coffee**	3 teaspoons
30 ml	**water**	2 tablespoons
4	**egg whites**	4
100 g	**caster sugar**	4 oz

The mousse can be made several hours in advance and kept in a refrigerator until required.

Grate the chocolate and keep a little on one side for the decoration. Put the remaining chocolate, coffee and water into a bowl standing over a pan of hot, not boiling water. Stir occasionally until the chocolate is melted and the mixture is smooth. Whisk the egg whites until they stand in peaks. Whisk in half the sugar and continue whisking until it is just as stiff again. Fold in the remaining sugar and the chocolate mixture, using a figure of eight movement so that the minimum amount of air is knocked out of the egg whites. Make quite sure that all the egg white is folded in and does not show. Carefully divide between 4–6 glasses and sprinkle over the grated chocolate.

Serves 4–6

Masked Coffee Cups

Illustrated on page 99

Metric		Imperial
500 ml	**milk**	1 pint
50 g	**semolina**	2 oz
15 ml	**instant coffee**	1 tablespoon
100 g	**caster sugar**	4 oz
	Sauce	
50 g	**soft brown sugar**	2 oz
25 g	**Bournville cocoa**	1 oz
125 ml	**milk**	$\frac{1}{4}$ pint
5 125-ml capacity	**moulds, rinsed with cold water**	5 $\frac{1}{4}$-pint capacity

If suitable moulds are not available, cups may be substituted. Use old cups, or the oven-to-table ware ones are ideal. Cool the mixture a little before putting it in, to avoid breaking the cold pottery.

Warm the milk in a saucepan then sprinkle in the semolina, coffee and sugar. Bring to the boil, stirring continuously. Reduce the heat and continue stirring and cooking for a few minutes to thicken the semolina. Divide between the prepared moulds and leave to cool and set.

Measure all the sauce ingredients into a pan. Stir over a low heat to dissolve the sugar then boil for a couple of minutes until the sauce is as thick as you require. Serve the sauce hot or cold over the turned out Coffee Cups.

Serves 5

Bavarian Cream

Illustrated on page 83

If a plate or dish is sprinkled with a very little cold water before a pudding is turned out on to it, this makes the surface slippery and the pudding can be moved easily.

Metric		Imperial
2	**eggs, separated**	2
25 g	**caster sugar**	1 oz
100 g	**Bournville plain chocolate**	4 oz
250 ml	**milk**	½ pint
2.5 ml	**vanilla essence**	½ teaspoon
14 g	**gelatine**	½ oz
60 ml	**water**	3 tablespoons
125 ml	**whipping cream**	¼ pint
2	**crystallised violets**	2
750-ml	**jelly mould, rinsed out**	1½-pint
	with cold water	
	piping bag and star pipe	

Cream the egg yolks with the sugar until they are lighter in colour. Break up the chocolate and place it in a saucepan with the milk and vanilla essence. Whisk over a gentle heat until the chocolate has dissolved, without letting it boil. Whisk the milk into the egg yolks then return to the pan. Stir the custard over a gentle heat when the mixture should thicken enough to coat the back of the wooden spoon.

Dissolve the gelatine in the water and when quite liquid and clear, pour it into the chocolate custard. Leave in a cool place until the mixture begins to thicken. Whisk the egg whites stiffly and whip the cream. Fold one good spoonful of whipped cream and the egg whites into the mixture. Pour into the prepared mould and leave to set for several hours. Later turn the mould out on to a plate and decorate with remaining cream, piped in stars round the edge and on top. Finish with two crystallised violets—or use pieces of glacé cherry.

Serves 6

Dreamy Mocha Dessert

Illustrated opposite

Metric		Imperial
75 g	**soft margarine**	3 oz
75 g	**caster sugar**	3 oz
25 g	**Bournville cocoa, sieved**	1 oz
50 g	**hazelnuts or mixed nuts, chopped**	2 oz
1	**egg**	1
20 ml	**sherry**	1 tablespoon
20 ml	**top of the milk**	1 tablespoon
200 ml	**strong black coffee**	7 fl oz
	1 packet (8) trifle sponges	
	Decoration	
75 g	**soft margarine**	3 oz
175 g	**icing sugar, sieved**	6 oz
	vanilla essence	
25 g	**Bournville plain chocolate, grated**	1 oz
12	**hazelnuts, blanched**	12
	greaseproof paper	
1-kg	**loaf tin, greased**	2-lb
	piping bag and star pipe	

Fold a piece of greaseproof paper to fit the length of the tin, with the ends hanging out at either end. Grease the paper too. Cream the margarine and sugar until lighter in colour and texture. Beat in the sieved cocoa, chopped nuts and the egg. Keep the mixture on one side.

Mix the sherry and milk into the strong coffee. Dip 4 of the sponges into the coffee and lay them side by side on the base of the tin. Spread the cocoa mixture on top and to the sides. Dip the remaining sponges in coffee and press them level on top. Chill overnight.

To make the decoration, cream together the margarine, sieved icing sugar and a few drops of vanilla essence, adding a little milk if necessary to make it a spreading consistency. Dip the tin in warm water and invert the dessert on to a suitable plate. Spread the icing on top. Fill the piping bag with the star pipe attached and pipe stars round the top and bottom of the loaf shape. Decorate with 3 lines of grated chocolate, hazelnuts down the centre and at each corner.

Serves 8

Paradise Ring (see page 105); Dreamy Mocha Dessert (see above); Masked Coffee Cups (see page 96)

good ✓

Banana Cream

Illustrated on page 119

Metric		Imperial
100 g	**Bournville plain chocolate**	4 oz
125 ml	~~double cream~~ *Cottage Cheese*	$\frac{1}{4}$ pint
125 ml	**natural yogurt**	$\frac{1}{4}$ pint
2	**large, very ripe bananas**	2

For a dinner party dessert, add 30 ml/2 tablespoons sherry.

Reserve two squares of chocolate. Melt the remainder in a bowl over a pan of hot water. Take off the heat and allow the melted chocolate to cool a bit. Whisk the cream and yogurt together until it will just hold its shape. Be careful not to over-whip the cream. Mash the bananas on a plate then fold them with the chocolate into the cream. Divide the cream between the glasses. Grate the remaining chocolate on top, covering the cream with quite a thick layer. Serve chilled.

Serves 4–5

Golden Crunch Layer

Illustrated on page 103

Metric		Imperial
75 g	**Bournville plain chocolate**	3 oz
100 g	**butter**	4 oz
60 ml	**golden syrup**	3 tablespoons
100 g	**icing sugar, sieved**	4 oz
1	**small orange**	1
175 g	**cornflakes**	6 oz
125 ml	**double cream**	$\frac{1}{4}$ pint
125 ml	**single cream**	$\frac{1}{4}$ pint
410-g can	**peach slices**	14$\frac{1}{2}$-oz can
2 18-cm	**round shallow cake tins, well greased**	2 7-inch
	piping bag and star pipe	

Break the chocolate into pieces and melt it with the butter and syrup in a large pan. Stir in the sieved icing sugar and the finely grated rind of the orange. Crush the cornflakes slightly before adding them too. Stir well so that they are completely coated in chocolate. Divide the mixture evenly between the tins, flattening it a little with a palette knife; avoid crushing it too much. Leave in a cold place for a couple of hours, or overnight. Segment the orange for the decoration.

Whip the double and single cream together until it will hold its shape. Warm the bases of the cake tins quickly to loosen the chocolate mixture. Turn out one layer on to a clean surface and the other on to the dish from which it will be served. Pipe whirls of cream at intervals round the chocolate layer on the table. Spread the remaining cream on to the other layer. Divide the peach slices and orange segments between the two layers. Lift the decorated layer on top of the other and eat within an hour.

Serves 6

Pears and Chocolate Sauce

Illustrated on page 103

For an easy and quick dessert, canned pear halves may be used. There is no comparison in the taste, especially when fresh pears are in season.

Metric		Imperial
200 g	**light soft brown or granulated sugar**	8 oz
550 ml	**water**	1 pint
	juice of $\frac{1}{2}$ orange or lemon	
5-cm	**piece of cinnamon stick**	2-inch
6	**dessert pears**	6
	Sauce	
100 g	**Bournville plain chocolate**	4 oz
25 g	**butter**	1 oz
15 ml	**rum**	1 tablespoon
25 g	**soft brown sugar**	1 oz
15 ml	**lemon juice**	1 tablespoon
15–30 ml	**pear juice**	1–2 tablespoons
1	**large block vanilla ice cream**	1

Dissolve the sugar in the water in a deep pan then boil for about 2 minutes with the fruit juice and cinnamon stick added. Thinly peel the pears, leaving the stalks on where possible. Stand the pears upright in the syrup and poach them gently for about 15 minutes until they are tender. Tilt the lid on the pan to prevent all the water evaporating but do not allow it to boil over. Turn the pears occasionally so that they are cooked on all sides. Leave them to cool in the syrup.

To make the sauce, break the chocolate into a saucepan. Stir in the butter, rum, sugar, lemon juice and the pear juice. Heat gently until the chocolate has melted then, stirring continuously, bring the sauce to the boil and simmer for a minute. Put spoonsful of ice cream round the pears in individual dishes and pour the chocolate sauce over the top.

Serves 6

Snowy Chocolate Ring

Illustrated opposite

Metric		Imperial
25 g	**Bournville cocoa**	1 oz
100 g	**soft margarine**	4 oz
200 g	**caster sugar**	8 oz
	few drops of vanilla essence	
3	**eggs**	3
100 g	**self-raising flour, sieved**	4 oz
425-g can	**black cherries**	15-oz can
80 ml	**kirsch**	4 tablespoons
142 ml	**whipping cream**	¼ pint
750-ml	**ring mould tin, well greased**	1½ pint

Blend the cocoa with just enough boiling water to make it into a thick paste. Cream the margarine with half the sugar until they are lighter in colour and texture. Add the vanilla essence. Beat in one whole egg and two egg yolks, reserving the whites for the meringue topping. Add the cocoa, then fold in the sieved flour. Turn into the prepared tin, level off the surface and bake in a moderately hot oven (190°C, 375°F, Gas Mark 5) for about 35 minutes. Leave the cake in the tin for a few minutes then loosen the edges and turn out on to a wire tray.

Drain the cherries but keep the juice. Stone the fruit. Place the cake upside down on an ovenproof plate that is big enough to allow the meringue as well. Soak the cake with kirsch and the cherry juice, pricking it with a skewer to allow the liquid to be absorbed properly. Leave for about an hour if possible. Whip the cream, fold in the stoned cherries and chill.

Fill the cake with the cream and spread the rest on top. Whisk the egg whites to the stiffness of meringue, fold in half the remaining sugar and whisk again until it will stand in peaks. Fold in all the sugar. Completely cover the cake with meringue, leaving no gaps at all. Bake in a very hot oven (230°C, 450°F, Gas Mark 8) for about 5 minutes until tinged with brown. Alternatively the dessert may be popped under a hot grill but the sides will not brown evenly. Serve immediately.

Serves 6

The cake should be frozen without the cream filling or meringue topping. Wrap, label and seal. Defrost the cake before filling and covering.

To make this a more traditional Baked Alaska, fill the centre with scoops of ice cream and pile the cherries on top before covering with meringue. The cake may crack on top when baking but this does not matter.

Snowy Chocolate Ring (see above); Golden Crunch Layer (see page 100); Cherry Cascade (see page 104); Pears and Chocolate Sauce (see page 101)

Cherry Cascade

Illustrated on page 103

Metric		Imperial
1 packet	**sponge fingers**	1 packet
425-g can	**red cherries**	15-oz can
20 ml	**cherry brandy**	1 tablespoon
375 ml	**milk**	$\frac{3}{4}$ pint
30 g	**Bournville cocoa**	1 oz
50 g	**caster sugar**	2 oz
2	**eggs, separated**	2
14 g	**gelatine**	$\frac{1}{2}$ oz
40 ml	**water**	2 tablespoons
	angelica pieces	
1-kg	**loaf tin**	2-lb

If the custard does curdle, blend 10 ml/2 teaspoons of custard powder with a little milk. Add the curdled custard, return to the pan and bring to the boil, stirring continuously. If it is very bad, it may be necessary to whisk the mixture too.

Arrange the sponge fingers, sugar side downwards, in the base of the tin. You will need about 10, depending on the actual size of your tin. Drain the cherries and pour 125 ml/$\frac{1}{4}$ pint of the juice, mixed with the cherry brandy, over the fingers. Warm the milk, cocoa and sugar together then beat in the egg yolks. Stir with a wooden spoon and cook the custard gently until it thickens enough to coat the back of the spoon. Do not allow it to boil or it may curdle. Cool the custard. Meanwhile stone the cherries.

Dissolve the gelatine in the water and when it is quite clear, stir into the custard. Ideally the custard and gelatine should be at the same warm temperature. As the custard cools, it should thicken and when it does, fold in the stoned cherries, reserving some for the decoration. Whisk the egg whites stiffly and fold in so that there are no patches of white left, then pour the mixture into the tin. Chill until firm. Later turn the dessert on to an oblong plate and decorate with cherries in the shape of a flower, using angelica pieces for the stalks and leaves. Extra cherries may be arranged round the dessert if liked. Serve with single cream.

Serves 6–8

Paradise Ring

Illustrated on page 99

The sponge fingers and cake may be frozen but not the assembled pudding.

This can be made with plain bought sponge fingers but the softer texture of home-made ones complement the chocolate mousse better. Gelatine mixtures tend to toughen in the refrigerator and are therefore better left to set in some other cool place.

Metric		Imperial
20	home-made Chocolate Sponge Fingers (see page 44)	20
I 18-cm	round sponge cake (see Whisked Sponge, page 85)	I 7-inch
150 g	Bournville plain chocolate	6 oz
4	eggs, separated	4
15 ml	instant coffee	2 teaspoons
14 g	gelatine	$\frac{1}{2}$ oz
80 ml	water	4 tablespoons
125 ml	double cream	$\frac{1}{4}$ pint
80 ml	single cream or top of the milk	4 tablespoons
25 g	Bournville plain chocolate	I oz
20-cm	round loose-based cake tin	8-inch
at least 1 metre	pretty ribbon	at least $1\frac{1}{4}$ yards
	piping bag and star pipe	

Oil the cake tin lightly. Cut the ends off the sponge fingers so that they are all more or less the same size. Place the sponge cake in the centre of the tin then pack the sponge fingers in the gap round the edge, flat side on the tin. Melt the chocolate in a fairly large bowl over a pan of hot water then stir in the egg yolks and the instant coffee. Dissolve the gelatine in the water without boiling and when it is quite clear, pour into the chocolate mixture. Leave to cool slightly. Whisk the egg whites stiffly and fold into the chocolate mixture. Turn the mixture into the prepared tin and leave for several hours to set, not in a refrigerator.

Lightly whip the creams or top of the milk together until it will just hold its shape. Melt the small amount of chocolate. Spread cream over the chocolate mousse in the tin and drop in the chocolate, swirling it with a skewer to give a marbled effect. Carefully push up the base of the tin then slide the pudding on to a plate. Tie the ribbon round the sponge fingers which will help to keep them in place. Pipe any remaining cream round the base.

Serves 6–8

Chocolate Ice Cream and Sauce

Illustrated opposite

Metric		Imperial
4	**egg yolks**	4
100 g	**caster sugar**	4 oz
550 ml	**milk**	1 pint
75 g	**Bournville plain chocolate**	3 oz
5 ml	**vanilla essence**	1 teaspoon
125 ml	**double cream**	$\frac{1}{4}$ pint
	Sauce	
50 g	**Bournville plain chocolate**	2 oz
80 ml	**golden syrup**	4 tablespoons
	knob of butter	
	ice cream wafer biscuits	

🚫

If the sauce gets cold, it will thicken. Heat to melt it again.

Make the custard in a double boiler if possible. Otherwise, it must be cooked over a very slow heat so that the eggs do not curdle.

Beat the eggs and sugar together in the top of a double boiler. Add the milk and cook until the custard thickens, stirring occasionally. Grate the chocolate into the custard, add the vanilla essence and whisk until smooth. Cool the custard. Whip the cream, fold into the cold egg custard and pour into an ice cube tray, or a metal container. Place in a food freezer or the freezing compartment of the refrigerator. Beat the mixture two or three times before it hardens, to remove large ice crystals and make a smooth consistency. An ice cream maker used in the freezer avoids the necessity for any beating. Serve the ice cream with the chocolate sauce and ice cream wafers.

To make the sauce, break the chocolate into squares and heat with the syrup and butter. Leave until smooth then beat quickly. Serve over the scoops of ice cream.

Serves 6–8

Chocolate Chip Ice Cream

Metric		Imperial
1 quantity	**Chocolate Ice Cream**	1 quantity
100 g	**Bournville plain chocolate**	4 oz
4	**small Cadbury's Flakes**	4

Make up the chocolate ice cream. Add the chocolate, chopped into small pieces before freezing. Serve with a Flake.

Chocolate Ice Cream and Sauce (see above); Nutty Chocolate Ice Cream (see page 108); Orange and Chocolate Ice Cream (see page 108); Ice Cream Pyramid (see page 108)

Nutty Chocolate Ice Cream

Illustrated on page 107

Metric		Imperial
1 quantity	**Chocolate Ice Cream**	1 quantity
100 g	**walnuts, halved**	4 oz

Make up the chocolate ice cream. Reserve a few of the best walnut halves for the top, chop the remainder and add to the ice cream before freezing. Serve with an ice cream wafer.

Ice Cream Pyramid

Illustrated on page 107

Metric		Imperial
1 quantity	**Chocolate Ice Cream and Sauce**	1 quantity
	sponge flan case	
6–8	**meringue halves**	6–8

Fill the sponge flan case with scoops of ice cream. Dot meringue halves over the top and pour on the chocolate sauce. For an easy alternative sauce melt 40 ml/2 tablespoons Cadbury's chocolate spread with 10 ml/2 teaspoons water.

Serves 6–8

Orange and Chocolate Ice Cream

Illustrated on page 107

Metric		Imperial
3	**egg yolks**	3
75 g	**caster sugar**	3 oz
275 ml	**milk**	$\frac{1}{2}$ pint
3	**oranges**	3
75 g	**Bournville plain chocolate**	3 oz
5 ml	**vanilla essence**	1 teaspoon
125 ml	**double cream**	$\frac{1}{4}$ pint

Stir the egg yolks and sugar together in the top of a double boiler, or cook in a pan over an extremely slow heat. Add the milk and cook the custard, stirring gently until it thickens enough to coat the back of a wooden spoon. Do not let the custard get too hot or it will curdle.

Choose oranges with good skins. Carefully squeeze out the juice; there should be about 275 ml/½ pint. If not, make it up with concentrated orange drink. Retain the orange shells. Melt the chocolate in the orange juice and vanilla essence over a gentle heat. Do not let it get too hot. Pour the liquid into the egg custard and cool. Later, whip the cream and fold in. Pour into an ice cube tray or metal container and freeze. Beat several times before it hardens.

Scoop the ice cream into the orange shells—it can also be served on its own. Return to the freezer until required. Decorate with a chocolate leaf or perhaps a scented geranium leaf.

Serves about 6

Sponge Flan Case

Pack carefully, preferably in foil or a rigid container so that the shape is retained. Label and seal.

If there is any difficulty in getting the sponge flan out of the tin, place the tin straight out of the oven on to a wet dish cloth. This helps the sponge to shrink quickly and come away from the tin.

Metric		Imperial
50 g	**caster sugar**	2 oz
2	**eggs**	2
50 g	**plain flour**	2 oz
15 g	**Bournville cocoa**	½ oz
20-cm	**sponge flan tin**	8-inch
	greaseproof paper	

The new silicone-lined flan tins are ideal to use in this recipe as they will turn out easily. Cut a circle of greaseproof paper to fit the centre and grease the tin and paper circle.

Whisk the sugar and eggs together in a bowl over a pan of hot water, or use an electric mixer. Whisk until the mixture is thick enough to write three letters, trailing it from the whisk. The first one should still be visible when the last one is written. Sieve the flour with the cocoa twice—this is important as the cocoa must be mixed in properly. Fold the dry ingredients carefully into the whisked eggs and sugar and turn into the flan tin. Bake in a fairly hot oven (200°C, 400°F, Gas Mark 6) for about 12 minutes until cooked. Turn out and cool on a wire tray, removing the paper from the centre.

The flan keeps quite well in an airtight tin. Fill the centre and use as required.

Baked Marbled Cheesecake

Metric		Imperial
	Base	
100 g	**plain flour**	4 oz
	pinch of salt	
50 g	**caster sugar**	2 oz
50 g	**margarine**	2 oz
	Filling	
100 g	**Bournville plain chocolate**	4 oz
300 g	**cream cheese**	12 oz
150 g	**caster sugar**	6 oz
50 g	**plain flour**	2 oz
5 ml	**vanilla essence**	1 teaspoon
4	**eggs**	4
142-ml carton	**natural yogurt**	5-fl oz carton
20-cm	**round loose-based cake tin, greased**	8-inch

Sieve the flour with a pinch of salt. Stir in the sugar and rub in the margarine. Press the mixture together then press it on to the base of the tin. Bake in a fairly hot oven (200°C, 400°F, Gas Mark 6) for 10 minutes.

Melt the chocolate in a small bowl over a pan of hot water. Beat the cream cheese with the sugar in a large bowl then blend in the flour and vanilla essence. Beat in the eggs one at a time and finally add the yogurt. Pour half the filling over the base. Mix the melted chocolate into the remainder and drop in spoonsful over the vanilla filling. Lightly swirl the two colours together to give a marbled effect. Lower the oven temperature and bake in a warm oven (160°C, 325°F, Gas Mark 3) for 1 hour. Turn off the oven and leave the cheesecake in it for a further hour. Take out of the tin when cold.

Serves 6–8

This cheesecake freezes well. Wrap in foil or waxed paper and a polythene bag. Seal, label and freeze.

The top may crack but this often happens with baked cheesecakes.

Cherry and Chocolate Meringue (see page 113); Meringue Cascade (see page 116); Mont Blanc Nests (see page 112); Chocolate Meringues (see page 114)

Mont Blanc Nests

Illustrated on page 111

Metric		Imperial
	Meringue nests	
2	**egg whites**	2
100 g	**caster sugar**	4 oz
	Filling	
100 g	**Bournville plain chocolate**	4 oz
2	**medium oranges**	2
225 g	**sweetened chestnut purée**	8 oz
125 ml	**double cream**	$\frac{1}{4}$ pint
80 ml	**single cream or**	4 tablespoons
	top of the milk	
	baking tray covered with	
	Bakewell paper	
	piping bag and star vegetable pipe	
	plain icing pipe	

A dry pastry brush is useful for brushing off the orange rind from the grater. If you want to use one orange only, peel the grated orange half that has not been squeezed and decorate the nests with half a slice each.

Draw six or seven circles measuring about 6 cm/2½ inches in diameter on the back of the paper, leaving some space between them. Use a felt tipped pen so the lines will show through.

Whisk the egg whites really stiffly. Fold in half the sugar and whisk again until they are as stiff. Fold in the remaining sugar. Fill the piping bag, with the star pipe attached, with meringue and pipe a spiral inside each marked circle, working from the centre towards the outside. Pipe round the outside edge twice more, making an edge for the nest. There will be either six or seven, depending on the size of the egg whites. Dry out the nests in a very cool oven (110°C, 225°F, Gas Mark ¼) for at least 4 hours. When the top has quite set and is firm enough to handle, the nests may be lifted carefully and turned over to dry on the other side.

Break the chocolate into squares and melt it in a basin over a pan of hot water. Grate one orange finely and add the rind to the chocolate, with about 40 ml/2 tablespoons of the orange juice. Mash the chestnut purée into the mixture, making a smooth consistency. Fill the piping bag again, this time with a small plain pipe attached, then pipe the mixture unevenly into the meringue cases. Alternatively, use a spoon. Whip the creams together and pile a spoonful on top of each meringue nest. Decorate with a thin slice of orange curled on top.

Makes 6 or 7 nests

Cherry and Chocolate Meringue

Illustrated on page 111

Illustrated on page 111

The meringue shell will store well in a large airtight container.

Granulated sugar can easily be ground down in a blender to use as caster sugar for this type of recipe.

Metric		Imperial
	Meringue case	
3	**egg whites**	3
75 g	**caster sugar**	3 oz
75 g	**icing sugar**	3 oz
40 ml	**Bournville cocoa**	2 tablespoons
	Filling	
100 g	**Bournville plain chocolate**	4 oz
75 g	**cake crumbs**	3 oz
50 g	**ground almonds**	2 oz
425-g can	**black cherries**	15-oz can
60 ml	**cherry brandy or**	4 tablespoons
	cherry juice	
275 ml	**double cream**	$\frac{1}{2}$ pint

large baking tray covered

with Bakewell paper

piping bag and star pipe

Mark a 26-cm/10$\frac{1}{2}$-inch circle on the covered baking tray. Whisk the egg whites really stiffly then add the caster sugar and whisk again until it is as stiff. Fold in the icing sugar and cocoa sieved together. Fill the piping bag and pipe a continuous spiral to fill the space inside the marked circle. Pipe a second layer of overlapping loops round the outer edge, to make a raised edge. Bake the meringue case in the lowest possible oven (110°C, 225°F, Gas Mark $\frac{1}{4}$) for about 5 hours, or overnight so that the meringue sets. It may be slightly soft in the middle but this does not really matter.

Grate the chocolate coarsely. Mix half of it with the cake crumbs and ground almonds. Melt the remaining grated chocolate and spread it inside the meringue case. Drain the cherries, reserve 8 or 9 cherries for the top and stone the remainder. Place the stoned cherries on top of the chocolate. Pile the cake crumb mixture on top and moisten it with the cherry brandy, or use cherry juice. Press it down slightly to make a fairly firm and flat top. Whip the cream until it will just hold its shape. Spread most of the cream over the top. Pipe a border round the edge and rosettes in the meringue loops. Arrange a whole cherry on top of each. Cut into about 10 pieces.

Serves 10

Chocolate Meringues

Illustrated on page 111

Metric		Imperial
3	**egg whites**	3
75 g	**caster sugar**	3 oz
75 g	**icing sugar**	3 oz
25 g	**Bournville cocoa**	1 oz
	Decoration	
125 ml	**double cream**	$\frac{1}{4}$ pint
3	**Cadbury's Flakes**	3
4	**glacé cherries**	4
12	**paper cake cases**	12

large piping bag and star	
vegetable pipe	
baking tray covered with	
Bakewell paper	

Using a mixture of caster and icing sugar produces a really smooth and crumbly meringue.

Whisk the egg whites really stiffly (see photograph 1, opposite). An electric mixer is ideal to use as it aerates the egg whites well and therefore gives a larger volume. Add the caster sugar and continue whisking so that the meringue is as stiff again. Sieve the icing sugar and cocoa together and fold in (see photograph 2, opposite). At this stage, the mixture becomes rather dry but it will all mix in. Fill the piping bag and pipe rosettes on the prepared tray (see photograph 3, opposite). Make between 20 and 24; the exact number depends on the size of the eggs. Cook the meringues in a very cool oven (130°C, 250°F, Gas Mark $\frac{1}{2}$) for about 1 hour then lower the heat to the lowest possible temperature for another 4 or 5 hours to dry out the meringues. Lift them off the paper and store in an airtight tin until required.

Whip the cream with a little top of the milk if preferred, until it will just hold its shape. Place a pair of meringues into a paper case then pipe or spread cream in between (see photograph 4, opposite). Decorate with a piece of Flake, cutting each one into three pieces, and small pieces of cherry. Pair all the meringues in the same way.

Makes 10–12 meringue pairs

1 Whisk the egg whites as stiffly as possible until standing in peaks and almost dry in consistency.

2 With a metal spoon, fold in the Bournville cocoa and icing sugar, sieved together, using a figure-of-eight movement.

3 Hold the filled piping bag upright and pipe even-sized rosettes on the prepared baking tray.

4 Pair the meringues, place the pairs in the paper cases and pipe cream between them.

Meringue Cascade

Illustrated on page 111

Metric		Imperial
3	**egg whites**	3
75 g	**caster sugar**	3 oz
75 g	**icing sugar, sieved**	3 oz
10 ml	**instant coffee powder**	2 teaspoons
	Crème au beurre	
150 g	**unsalted butter**	6 oz
150 g	**granulated sugar**	6 oz
75 ml	**water**	2 fl oz
3	**egg yolks**	3
150 g	**Bournville plain chocolate**	6 oz

large baking tray covered
with Bakewell paper
piping bag and star pipe

To make Gâteau Diane: divide the meringue mixture between three 15-cm/6-inch circles. Layer them up with the crème au beurre and decorate with stars piped round the top. 50 g/2 oz of finely ground roasted hazelnuts may also be added to the uncooked meringue.

Always use fresh egg whites to make meringues. If they have been kept in the refrigerator, allow them to come to room temperature before using.

Whisk the egg whites really stiffly. Mix the caster sugar and the sieved icing sugar together. Add half the sugar and continue whisking until the mixture is as stiff again. Fold in the remaining sugar. Fill the piping bag with half the meringue and pipe whirls on to the prepared tray. Fold the coffee powder in to the remaining meringue and pipe on to the baking tray too. They spread slightly more than the plain meringues. Dry out the meringues in a very cool oven (110°C, 225°F, Gas Mark ¼) for about 4 hours until they are firm and will lift off easily. Store the meringues in an airtight container until they are required.

Make the special chocolate butter cream by softening the butter and beating it in a bowl. Dissolve the sugar in the water over gentle heat, in a saucepan. When all the granules have disappeared, boil rapidly until the short thread stage is reached. To test this, oil your first finger and thumb, dip a spoon in to the boiling syrup and touch it. When it is ready, you should be able to draw out a short thread before it breaks. It is important that this stage is reached otherwise the crème au beurre will not thicken enough.

Beat the egg yolks together using an electric mixer if available. Pour on the sugar syrup very slowly and continue beating as the mixture thickens and becomes much paler in colour. When all the syrup has been added, beat in the butter a spoonful at a time. Melt all but 50 g/2 oz of the chocolate in a bowl over hot water and add this too. The crème au beurre may now be left in the refrigerator for several days if necessary.

To assemble the dessert, spread the meringues with the chocolate crème au beurre which should not be too cold or it will be difficult to handle. Pile them up on an attractive dish, mixing the plain and coffee meringues. Grate the remaining chocolate and sprinkle it liberally over the top. The dessert may be assembled the day ahead and is nice to eat when it is slightly softer.

Serves at least 8

Silky Crunch Pie

Substitute Cadbury's dairy milk chocolate for the Bournville plain chocolate if a milk chocolate flavour is preferred.

Metric		Imperial
	Biscuit crust base	
175 g	digestive biscuits	6 oz
50 g	butter	2 oz
25 g	caster sugar	1 oz
	Filling	
25 g	butter	1 oz
25 g	cornflour	1 oz
25 g	caster sugar	1 oz
375 ml	milk	$\frac{3}{4}$ pint
75 g	Bournville plain chocolate	3 oz
	Decoration	
125 ml	double cream	$\frac{1}{4}$ pint
	small packet Cadbury's Buttons	
18-cm	shallow dish	7-inch
	piping bag and star pipe	

Crush the biscuits but do not make them too fine as this makes the crust rather dense and heavy. Melt the butter in a saucepan. Stir in the crushed biscuits and the sugar. Press the mixture on to the base and up the sides of the dish.

Melt the butter for the filling, in a saucepan. Blend in the cornflour with the sugar then gradually add the milk. Stir continuously while bringing the sauce to the boil and cook for a couple of minutes to thicken. Take the pan off the heat. Break up the chocolate and stir it into the hot sauce until melted. Pour the filling into the biscuit crust and leave it to set.

Whip the cream until it will hold its shape. Pipe rosettes round the edge of the pudding and decorate with the Buttons.

Serves 5–6

Ice Mountain

Illustrated opposite

Metric		Imperial
200 g	**Bournville plain chocolate**	8 oz
40 ml	sugar	2 tablespoons
60 ml	**lime juice cordial**	3 tablespoons
12	**trifle sponges, or**	12
250 g	sponge cake	9 oz
2	**eggs, separated**	2
125 ml	**double cream**	$\frac{1}{4}$ pint
125 ml	**single cream**	$\frac{1}{4}$ pint
1.5-litre	**pudding basin**	$2\frac{1}{2}$-pint

Reserve two squares of chocolate. Melt the remainder in a basin over a pan of hot water, with the sugar and lime juice. Meanwhile split all the trifle sponges in half to make thin pieces. Line the basin with the soft spongy side of the cake on the outside. Fill in the gaps with pieces of cake cut to fit. When the chocolate has melted, add the egg yolks, making sure the mixture is not too hot. Whisk the egg whites stiffly. In a separate bowl, whip half the amount of both creams together quite stiffly. Add the chocolate to the cream then fold in the whisked egg whites. Spoon some of the mixture into the basin covering the sponge in the bottom. Arrange a layer of sponge on top, again filling in the gaps. Repeat these processes, ending with sponge. All the chocolate mixture should be used up. Put a plate on top, the same size as the top of the bowl. Press it down with weights. Leave in the refrigerator for a day.

Ease a knife down the sides of the bowl then turn out the pudding on to a plate. Whip the remaining cream and spread it quite thinly over the pudding. Cover with grated chocolate. Cut into about 6 wedges.

Serves 6–7

Fondue (see page 82); Chocolate Sponge Fingers (see page 44); Ice Mountain (see above); Banana Cream (see page 100)

SWEETS AND CANDIES

Sweet making has become rather a specialised hobby and there are several complete books devoted to the subject. We are lucky enough to have a very high standard of confectionery and sugar products available from manufacturers, and Cadbury's is one of the largest. The high degree of technology and skill involved in tempering chocolate or getting the sugar boil right, takes years to perfect. Coating fondants smoothly with chocolate, pulling sugar and making Easter eggs are better left to the experts. We have therefore not tried to compete with commercial confectionery and have given recipes here that can easily be made at home, without any special equipment.

Nut Fudge

Metric		Imperial
50 g	**butter**	2 oz
25 g	**Bournville cocoa**	1 oz
80 ml	**water**	4 tablespoons
40 ml	**honey**	2 tablespoons
450 g	**granulated sugar**	1 lb
200 g	**condensed milk**	7 oz
50 g	**hazelnuts or walnuts,**	2 oz
	roughly chopped	
18-cm	**square shallow cake tin,**	7-inch
	lightly oiled	

Measure the butter, cocoa, water, honey, sugar and condensed milk into a fairly large pan. Stir over a low heat until the sugar has completely dissolved. Bring the mixture to the boil and cook steadily but not too fiercely, until the soft ball stage is reached. This will be 114°C/238°F on a sugar thermometer. An easy test is to have a saucerful of cold water ready. Drop a little fudge off the spoon into the water; when it is ready, it will form a soft ball and not break up between your fingers. Take the pan off the heat immediately then beat hard with a wooden spoon until the fudge becomes smooth in texture and thickens. Stir the roughly chopped nuts into the fudge. Pour into the tin and smooth over the surface. Leave to set overnight. Cut into squares.

Makes 36 pieces

Almond Candies

A few drops of rum essence or 10 ml/2 teaspoons of liqueur can be kneaded into the almond paste, especially at Christmas time or when the candies are to be made for a gift.

Metric		Imperial
100 g	almond paste	4 oz
25 g	small seedless raisins	1 oz
	icing sugar	
100 g	Cadbury's dairy milk or	4 oz
	Bournville plain chocolate	
5	red and green glacé cherries, halved	5
9	sweet paper cases	9

Knead the almond paste to soften it. If it is really hard, it may help to warm it in the oven. Knead in the raisins. Divide the paste into 9 equal-sized pieces then roll each one into a ball, dusting them with icing sugar if they are at all sticky. Melt the chocolate in a bowl over a pan of hot water. Dip the candies into the melted chocolate, covering the top half. Pop them into the paper cases, with the chocolate on top. Stick half a cherry on each, mixing the colours. Leave the chocolate to dry.

Makes 9 candies

Quick Chocolate Fudge

Illustrated on page 123

Metric		Imperial
100 g	Bournville plain chocolate	4 oz
50 g	butter	2 oz
30 ml	milk	2 tablespoons
5 ml	vanilla essence	1 teaspoon
425 g	icing sugar	1 lb
18-cm	square shallow tin,	7-inch
	lightly greased	

Break up the chocolate and melt it with the butter in a bowl placed over a pan of hot water. Stir occasionally to help the chocolate to soften. Take the bowl off the heat. Stir in the milk and vanilla essence then gradually beat in the icing sugar, sieving it as you do so. Blend thoroughly before turning the fudge into the prepared tin. Level the surface with a knife. Leave the fudge to get cold then cut into squares.

Makes 36 pieces

Chocolate Caramels

Metric		Imperial
50 g	**Cadbury's drinking chocolate**	2 oz
165 g	**golden syrup**	6 oz
225 g	**sugar**	8 oz
284 ml	**single cream**	$\frac{1}{2}$ pint
16-cm	**square shallow cake tin,**	$6\frac{1}{2}$-inch
	lightly oiled	

Use a heavy saucepan with a thick base for making sweets. Sugar reaches a high temperature but must not be allowed to burn as this will spoil the taste.

Measure the drinking chocolate, syrup, sugar and cream into a fairly large, heavy saucepan. Stir until the sugar has dissolved then bring slowly to the boil. Continue cooking gently for about 1 hour, leaving the pan uncovered. Do not allow the base to catch. Stir occasionally if necessary. The mixture will thicken considerably and reduce by half. Pour into the tin and leave to cool. Before it is quite hard, mark into squares. The caramels may be wrapped in squares of waxed or cellophane paper and stored in a dry place.

Makes 36 caramels

Coconut Ice

Illustrated opposite

Metric		Imperial
200 ml	**condensed milk**	8 tablespoons
325 g	**icing sugar**	12 oz
150 g	**desiccated coconut**	6 oz
	few drops of cochineal food colouring	
20 ml	**Bournville cocoa**	1 tablespoon
18-cm	**square cake tin, greased**	7-inch

The coconut ice is not too stiff. If a harder texture is preferred, add extra coconut or cocoa.

Mix the condensed milk and the icing sugar together in a bowl. Stir in the coconut. Divide the mixture in half. Add a few drops of the colouring slowly to one amount, making it pink. Spread this in the tin. Sieve the cocoa into the remaining mixture and stir in well. Spread on top of the pink coconut ice in the tin, levelling the surface. Leave overnight to set. Cut into squares.

Makes 36 pieces

Quick Chocolate Fudge (see page 121); Coconut Ice (see above); Surprise Bites (see page 124); Truffles (see page 124); Mallow Cherry Cushions (see page 126); Scrumptious Squares (see page 125)

Surprise Bites

Illustrated on page 123

Metric		Imperial
50 g	**butter**	1½ oz
30 ml	**Bournville cocoa**	2 tablespoons
90 ml	**condensed milk**	3 tablespoons
50 g	**soft brown sugar**	2 oz
175 g	**desiccated coconut**	6 oz
123-g packet	**marshmallows**	4.34-oz packet

Melt the butter in a saucepan. Add the cocoa, condensed milk and sugar and heat until melted, stirring continuously. Off the heat, add all but 25 g/1 oz of the coconut. Divide mixture equally into 15 and flatten the pieces between your hands. Mould this round the marshmallows, forming balls. Toss in the remaining coconut. Allow to harden slightly before they are eaten. Keep in an airtight container until required.

Makes 15

This is a recipe which children will enjoy making and find fairly easy to do.

Truffles

Illustrated on page 123

Metric		Imperial
150 g	**Bournville plain chocolate**	6 oz
40 ml	**brandy or fruit squash**	2 tablespoons
50 g	**unsalted butter**	1½ oz
60 g	**icing sugar, sieved**	2 oz
50 g	**ground almonds**	2 oz
8	**glacé cherries, halved**	8
16	**small sweet paper cases**	16

Break up two-thirds of the chocolate into a bowl and place this over a pan of hot water. Add the brandy and leave to melt. Take off the heat and stir in the butter, which should not be too hard. Mix in the sieved icing sugar and the almonds so that it is well blended. Leave in a cool place if necessary until the mixture is firm enough to handle. Divide into about 16 even-sized pieces and roll into balls. Grate the remaining chocolate, place on a piece of greaseproof paper and roll the truffles in it. Pop each one into a paper case and press half a cherry into the top.

Makes 16

Truffles may be frozen without the cherries but this is not usually necessary as they keep well in a cool place. The liquor taste and smell disappears in the freezer. Pack carefully, seal and label.

For a different effect, roll some of the truffles in Cadbury's drinking chocolate or Bournville cocoa.

Ruffled Robins

Metric		Imperial
1 quantity	**Truffles mixture**	1 quantity
5	**glacé cherries, halved**	5
25 g	**flaked almonds**	1 oz
	angelica pieces	

Divide the truffle mixture into 10 slightly larger balls. Roll them in grated Bournville plain chocolate. Stick half a glacé cherry on one side of each ball, with 2 flaked almonds just above for the 'beak'. Make 'tails' from the angelica.

Makes 10

Sweet. *Scrumptious Squares*

Illustrated on page 123

Metric		Imperial
	Base	
25 g	**caster sugar**	1 oz
125 g	**plain flour**	5 oz
100 g	**butter**	4 oz
	Filling	
100 g	**butter or margarine**	4 oz
100 g	**light soft brown sugar**	4 oz
40 ml	**golden syrup**	2 tablespoons
1	**small can condensed milk**	1
2.5 ml	**vanilla essence**	½ teaspoon
175 g	**Bournville plain chocolate**	6 oz
18-cm	**square shallow cake tin, greased**	7-inch

Add the sugar to the flour then rub in the butter until it resembles breadcrumbs. Knead slightly then press the shortbread mixture into the tin. Bake in a moderate oven (180°C, 350°F, Gas Mark 4) for 25 minutes. Cool in the tin.

Stir the butter, brown sugar, syrup and condensed milk together in a heavy based pan over a gentle heat, until dissolved. Now boil for 7 minutes but keep stirring to prevent the fudge catching on the bottom. Add the vanilla essence then beat with a wooden spoon, off the heat, until cool and shiny. Pour over the base in the tin. When cold, melt the chocolate in a bowl over hot water and spread over the fudge. When cool, cut into squares.

Makes 49

Mallow Cherry Cushions

Illustrated on page 123

Metric		Imperial
	Centre	
50 g	**butter**	2 oz
40 ml	**Bournville cocoa**	2 tablespoons
50 g	**icing sugar, sieved**	2 oz
25 g	**ground almonds**	I oz
15 ml	**brandy or sherry**	I tablespoon
	Outer layer	
50 g	**granulated sugar**	2 oz
50 g	**butter**	2 oz
30 ml	**water**	2 tablespoons
123-g packet	**marshmallows**	4.34-oz packet
100 g	**icing sugar, sieved**	4 oz
25 g	**walnuts, chopped**	I oz
25 g	**glacé cherries, chopped**	I oz

Sprinkle the surface with icing sugar when rolling out the sweets.

Make the centre first. Melt the butter in a saucepan and cook the cocoa in it. Take the pan off the heat and stir in the sieved icing sugar, ground almonds and the brandy. Chill the mixture so that it can harden.

Dissolve the granulated sugar in the butter and water over low heat and when it is quite clear, boil for about 5 minutes. Take the pan off the heat. Stir in the marshmallows and when they have melted, add the sieved icing sugar and the chopped walnuts and cherries, mixed together. Cool this mixture too. When it is cold and firm enough to handle, divide the mixture in half and roll into two strips, each measuring about 33 cm × 7.5 cm/13 inches × 3 inches. Halve the mixture for the centre too and form into two rolls the same length. Wrap the flat strips round the chocolate rolls, joining the edges by rolling them slightly. Cut each of the rolls in half, making four shorter ones. Wrap these individually in waxed or greaseproof paper and leave in the refrigerator to harden. Later cut into slices.

Makes 24

INDEX

Apricot Cream

8oz Fresh Apricots
3oz Pl Choc
4oz Cottage/Curd Cheese

Stew apricots in juice/water.
Cream cheeses, add apricots
Melt choc & combine.
Decorate with banana or choc buttons.